Massimiliano Fuksas (FRAMES)

By Doriana O. Mandrelli

For Elisa and Lavinia

FRAMES
MASSIMILIANO FUKSAS

I spent the day in Vienna, at the Twin Towers site,
which is now almost finished.
I've dreamt of building these towers for years.
The project, or rather the construction, seems not
to belong to me anymore. This is something that
happens at the end of every project. I become a
visitor like everyone else. I forget the details
and the arguments and I no longer remember the
difficulties. What I have left is the building.
From the great "trapezium-shaped base", 25 meters
of which is buried underground, to the highest
point, 150 meters up, the course I follow is
a journey through the constants that always exist
in an architect's work. The labyrinth prevails in
the lower part. The "parts" never come into
contact with each other as it is the void that
generates "tension".
It is an unpredictable journey in which different
heights and dimensions are discovered. The move
from "small" to "big", from ceilings that squash
you to others that are far away, can be found in
many of my projects.
Seen from the walkways that connect them, the two
towers are non-parallel monoliths that almost
touch each other. The closest point between them

is only six meters wide. The two bodies create an
"interstice". The architecture of interstices or
voids, existing between one object and the other,
is one of the constants that have "obsessed"
my architecture for about 25 years.
We move through different emotions in a series
of tensions and releases.
I went down thirty meters underground and
gradually allocated parking areas, cinemas,
restaurants, shops and offices. I tried to
organize the greater part of the public and
private life of many people in the same place.
What is particularly special about this building
is its maximum transparency.
Another world, a mysterious world, exists
underneath. The concept of a simple monolith,
with a world above and a world beneath it and a
"horizon", a recurring key word with which I have
replaced the concept of "stairs" as I consider
it too static. The horizon, on the other hand,
moves with the human being. You look at it
and change it by moving up and down, rather like
in a movie. Mankind draws its horizons through
its own movements, so it is casual like the choices
that are made.
Observing the flows, the casual dynamics,
the single choices. Observing space without

architecture and imagining only the tracks beaten
into the ground. Experiencing nocturnal visions,
during long flights, of cities that flow under
clear night skies, like "filaments", sources
of light, "spiders" that shatter in
a thousand directions to weave their net.
Removing everything and leaving only "the
songlines". Understanding the relationships
between these senses of travel. What is left
though, is not a void, it is a place.
It is an island that follows the path.
This time, elimination has given birth to
fullness, to matter that can still be modified,
not only section by section, but in all dimensions.
Islands accept the law of chance, the law of
chaos. They become a location where different
possibilities converge and thus, a place of
accumulation and events.
The islands become the location of the Inseln
project that is being used to expand the Europark
in Salzburg. The Europark II project is divided
into two parts: the expansion of the existing mall
and the landscape design of the area.
The landscape design is an analysis of paths,
which it organizes, creating artificial hills,
footpaths and raised areas. The islands, on the
other hand, are responsible for the structure of

the mall. They are spaces determined by the nature
of chance. Organized on two levels, the mall ends
with the covered parking area, on which potential,
fluid evolutions of the same basic "Inseln" expand
and become almost totems of the new building,
making it immediately recognizable.
50's art was full of triangular structures, where
all the sides were different, because they were
constructed using radiuses from different curves;
flux is similar to these radiuses and the result
is an object that is always different.
Variability characterizes every floor, up until
the last level where chaos explodes, takes over
and makes itself seen.
The complete acceptance of chaos and the
elimination of anything that tries to hide it,
belongs to the same process of thought which gave
rise to the study for the new Gallery of Modern
Art project. It also developed from the process
that began with the EUR Conference Center and is
better known as "Floating Space". The acceptance
of chaos, which to begin with was quite moderate,
is at this stage totally visible. The box no longer
exists. Disorder becomes structure.
Section by section, chaos carves out a space for
itself, hollows out and frees a place, transforms
it and transforms itself.

The Modern art gallery is all that is needed to
build and understand the EUR Conference Center.
The latter is its negative image, its
evolution. What remains of the cloud is the
element supporting the matter. It is strange
that it came later. The order is not direct
it is inverted.
By eliminating the box, anything that was
superfluous in the translucent EUR envelope
dissolved. Zevi has always criticized the type
of architecture that makes use of an opposite
structure to express the concept, the essential,
and he has never agreed with the manifestation
of process, of thesis and antithesis.
He has always demanded the demonstration of
synthesis only.
Structure is essential, perceivable, but the
buildings are not rhetorically, statically
visible, structure, in this case, represents the
transformation of chaos and its potential use.
The process is no longer shown, but the fact
that it can still be modified turns it into flux,
the so-called "Bergsonian flow", the flow of the
twentieth century conscience.
Tension is obtained by overcoming the phases of
logic. It is born deep down and then explodes,
perhaps even becoming a project.

As in Vienna, as in the attempt to make a monolith,
a space odyssey's prize, weightless.
This essential, recognizable and transparent
structure has lost all of its unknown and
mysterious features by becoming luminous and
light. In the foundations, however, the memory
of this suffering remains and in the Piranesian
view of inside space, the modernity that has now
become contemporary still lingers.
Two objects that do not touch, even if they
are rooted in the same ground and communicate via
a walkway that passes through the interstice.
This is the power of non-contact, of distance,
of concept.
Two changeable, iridescent knife edges that
at times become completely transparent, opaque,
or mirror-like and at others return to being
compact matter only to surrender again to the
lightness of glass.
Two monoliths, which are lost in the sky and at
the same time, stand out in that same space.
This is a place of opposites and contradictions,
solved through a sense of generous visual
accessibility. Intrigue and its resolution,
interval and its interruption. A pause between
two buildings, a caesura, union and unity,
the magic of freedom and the poetry of lightness.

Something that is born underground and then
sprouts powerfully in the city, losing intrigue
by acquiring a transparent mass, something that
flows deep inside and rushes vertically towards a
concept of the dignity and freedom of mankind,
a being who is able to change and create.
Tension, wish and desire come together to form two
objects as they rise from the depths. Two possible
worlds. Here, thesis and antithesis live together,
even if they remain separate and distant.
The world of the labyrinth and lost rationality
stays below, while purification reigns above.
Synthesis, concept? It is impossible to find
yourself in these projects where the means becomes
the end and then the end becomes the means.
Chance and the process of chance are the only
interesting phenomena.
The important thing is not the possibilities,
but how to bring them about.
What is important to us, the people who consciously
plan chance events, is our capacity to amaze and
be amazed, to surprise and be surprised.
We must always be able to wonder, to believe in
magic and even if we are the ones who create that
magic, we must never reveal the secret.

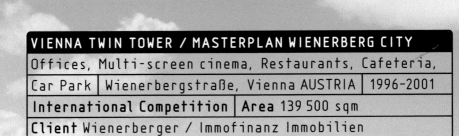

VIENNA TWIN TOWER / MASTERPLAN WIENERBERG CITY

Offices, Multi-screen cinema, Restaurants, Cafeteria,
Car Park | Wienerbergstraße, Vienna AUSTRIA | 1996–2001

International Competition | **Area** 139 500 sqm

Client Wienerberger / Immofinanz Immobilien

Tension, wish and desire come together to form two objects as they rise from the depths.
Two possible worlds. Here, thesis and antithesis live together, even if they remain separate and distant. The world of the labyrinth and lost rationality stays below, while purification reigns above.

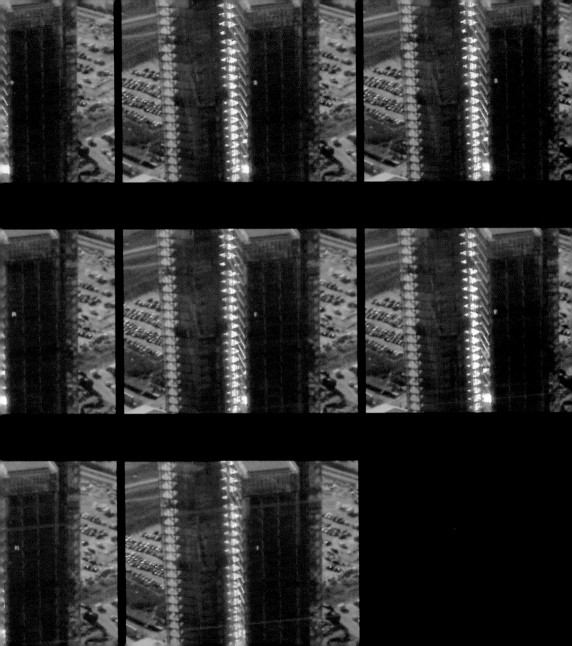

MASTERPLAN WIENERBERG CITY

From the beginning Fuksas's research has been based on the desire to pinpoint a solution that would enrich the skyline of the Austrian capital. Firstly, to give it greater depth, and then also to add an entire quarter, which will both complete the existing structure and act as a common element of identification for future users. Situated in an area where the city and the green areas meet, the project reunites and exalts themes that are already present in previous works. These include the development of the urban landscape; the connection-transition between urban density and green spaces; the studied confluence and reciprocal contamination of art and architecture; Land Art, in particular in the plaza to the south; the "ethical" dimension of the project on an urban scale that "re-reads" the infrastructure system of the new area in key terms such as "accessibility" and "transparency". Articulated sinuously on a "landscaped" street, the project utilizes various types of architecture - towers and lines – in order to avoid any hint of monotony in the entire complex and at the same time enabling all of the distributive elements of each constructed organism to be easily identifiable.

Master plan >

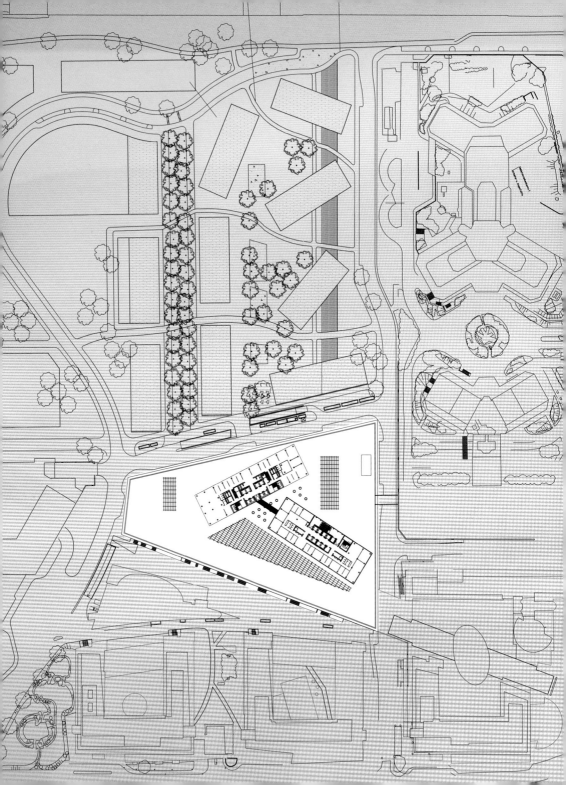

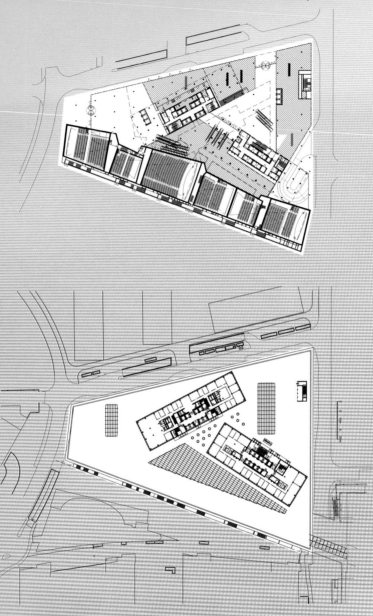

Ground floor plan

Typical floor plan

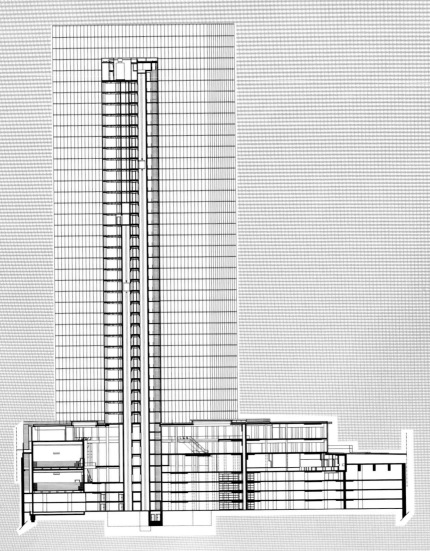

Cross section tower A

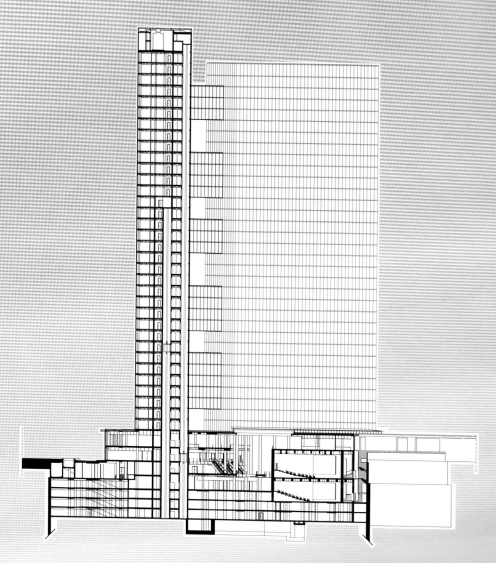

Cross section tower B

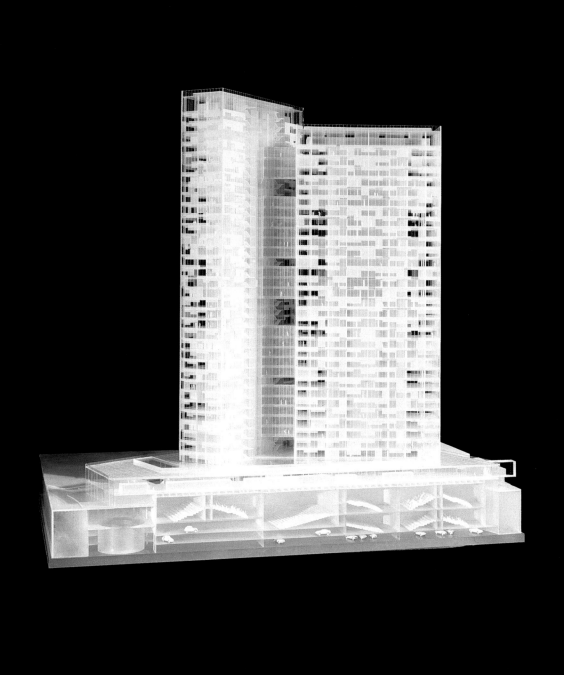

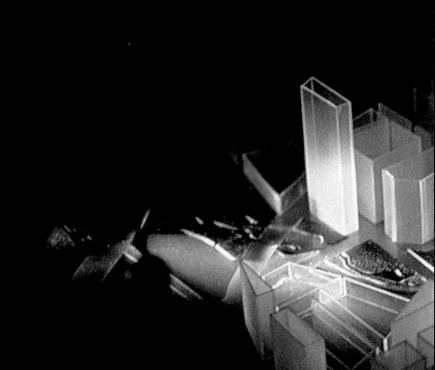

The starting point for this project is the creation of a system of overlapping networks capable of anticipating any future uncertainty. It is a highly significant program that aims to cater for any intensive development carried out in a number of different phases.

The proposal that can be formulated now will, in reality, undergo alteration inevitably. The plan is one that evolves constantly. It is much simpler to observe the present to understand the past. This is a concept that contains elements from the tradition and history of the Chinese people, such as the traditional Chinese house, with its framework based on the relationship between nature and construction. The history of Shanghai is very much a "frontier" history, very Chinese for the Europeans, and very European for the Chinese. I think that the concept put forward should be viewed as no more than a point of departure, an aid to imagining the future, a concept that will move, almost imperceptibly, inside the space destined to contain it.

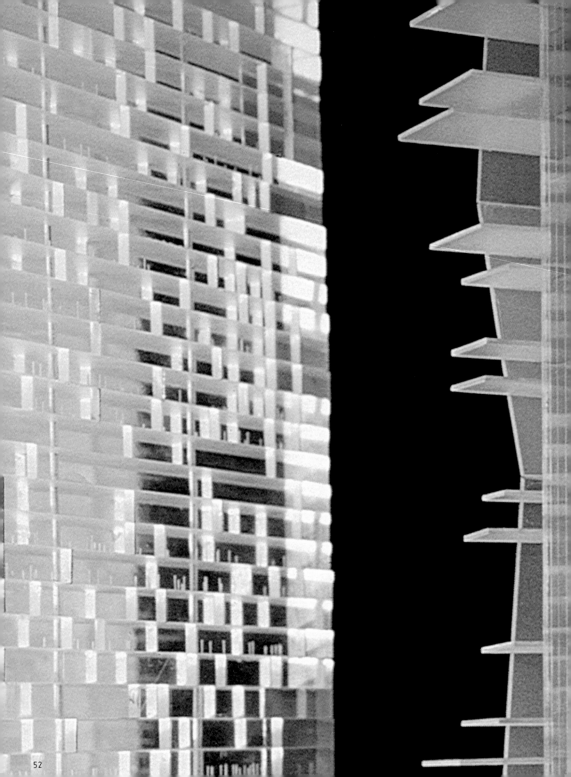

In the "Construction Training and Research Center"
in Alfortville, a suburb on the Seine, to the east
of Paris, a different procedure is used.
Here urban scale is replaced by the horizon,
which changes as one's viewpoint changes.
In places the ground level is raised even as high
as 7 meters and this changes one's view of the
tower blocks which make up the surrounding
landscape. In the Alfortville project, all I did
was to remove, cut and delete part of this 7 meter
high area. Carving, removing and cutting are
constants in my work and they are also present
in my two major Austrian projects, the Europark
canopy in Salzburg and the bases on which the twin
towers in Vienna rest. More recently, they can
also be seen in the EUR Conference Center in Rome,
in the new ASI head offices, again in Rome, and in
the Regional Council headquarters in Turin.
The almost radical project for the ASI is divided
into three identical portions. The complex
oscillates between extreme simplicity, created
by the "critical mass" of green (which colors
the other portions) and a vertical space
"sketched" by the continuity of a "ribbon".
The new Regional Council headquarters in Turin is
an extreme experiment. A 117 meter high void with

a number of suspended elements create a luminous, weightless space that is added to a simple "body". Obviously certain constants can be found in a number of different projects. They are nothing more than summaries of modes of expression, such as interstice, continuity, voids, horizon, geography, matter...

Many of my projects represent a move or the desire to move from one idea to another, until the moment arrives when it is time to move from design to construction.

In the Salzburg Europark project, as in many others, I was inspired by a film, *Point Break* by Catherine Bigelow, which tells the story of a group of surfers. The powerful character of the Europark canopy covers the car park and at the same time it is a call, a wave, a monument to freedom.

The continuity of this element is counterbalanced by the tense, dynamic arrangement of the shopping area "voids" beneath it.

My dream was to see people walking on the roof. It is a sort of anti shopping center, but it works very well nevertheless.

It is a place where people can meet and spend summer nights, even if only to drink something and admire the surrounding landscape.

The light passes through a platform that has been cut, sculpted and pierced, allowing days and seasons to project shadows and images on the floor. Objects rest lightly on the ground sketching out a new urban landscape.

The architectural concept behind this project follows its own logic. The first floor platform is the unifying element. It marks the vertical separation between the almost industrial world of the lofty teaching areas situated beneath it and the traditional upper level rooms that are divided, according to program requirements, by the volumes that rest upon it.

This building seeks to demonstrate its openness to the city and the urban spaces that are the natural continuation of its own architecture. This openness is reached through the rhythm of volumes and seams, such as the fully glazed height of some of the ground floor sections. Here the many and complex architectural spaces enable the building and the city to converse. The lack of a general recreational area on the ground floor is compensated by large spaces on the first floor. These, too, open towards the city. The building acts and reacts to its urban context. It has an active tendency to construct tense volumes in contrast to the rigid verticality of the neighboring buildings that narrow the horizon. Whereas when the urban morphology of the old town of Alfortville and the course of the river Seine impose their strict linearity, it reacts and only unfold when it follows the classic rhythm of its own facades.

MAXIMILIEN PERRET DE VINCENNES

College for the formation and research on construction

Library, Documentation Center, Auditorium, Professor and

Student residence halls | Altforville FRANCE | 1995–97

Competition | **Area** 28 000 sqm

Client Île de France Regional Council

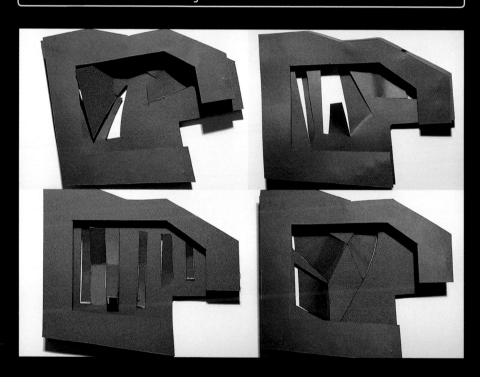

EUROPARK

Mall and Entertainment Center, Salzburg AUSTRIA	1994–97
International Competition	**Area** 150 000 sqm
Client SPAR Warenhandela AG, A-Salzburg	

The project, covering an area of 120 000 sqm of commercial space plus a parking area that holds 3 000 cars, is a suggestive allusion to one element that Austria does not possess, the sea. The powerful character of the canopy that covers the car park is also a large-scale motif. The continuity of this element is counterbalanced by the dynamic layout and the tension that the volumes beneath it are charged with. The force of the interior "voids" reserved for commercial activities determines this tension. In the southern part of this area, which is full of vegetation, the refined play of reflections created between the large walls, the serigraphed glass of the commercial center and the pool of water crossed by paths, demonstrate again Fuksas' unique constructive sensibility with regard to "light" and "transparency".

REDEVELOPMENT OF 'PIAZZA SHOPPING CENTER'

SHOPPING MALL AND OFFICE COMPLEX

Eindhoven THE NETHERLANDS	1999–2003
International Competition	**Area** 25 000 sqm
Client William Properties, Rotterdam	

The existing 70's shopping center will be redeveloped and enlarged to meet the needs of the present and future. The project is situated in the center of Eindhoven, which was rebuilt after the war next to the monumental Bijenkorf building designed by Gió Ponti. In the project the public walkway connecting the north and south parts of Eindhoven consists of a glass roof that extends over the square in front of the building. The four floors of the shopping center are connected by an elliptical void that brings natural light into the building. It is this void that gives the building its sense of spatial complexity, a complexity that can be understood in a single glance. Behind the façade, glazed in translucent green glass, stands a luminous sculpture. The new "piazza" and the Ponti building will together bring a totally new sense of scale to the city of Eindhoven.

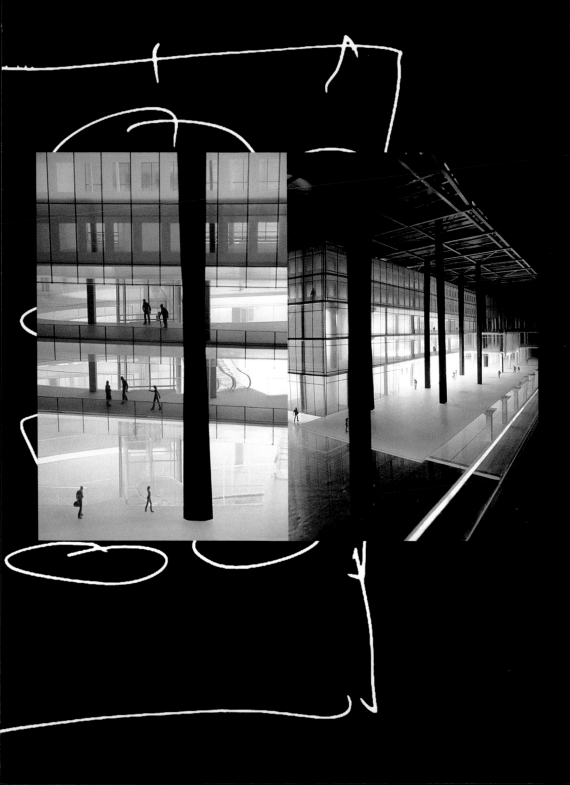

NEW FERRARI MANAGEMENT OFFICES
AND RESEARCH PLATFORM

Maranello ITALY | 2001–2002

Area 13 000 sqm | **Client** FERRARI S. p. A.

This project represents the development of a new poetic of lightness. Rather than a building, we can talk about the creation of a new landscape, a new geography: the water, the bamboo, the use of ecological materials, the extreme attention to biotechniques which make the working spaces more pleasant. The overall image is dominated by an overhanging volume, suspended above the surface of water that covers the first floor, as if it were flying. The surface of water is the space within which the various walkways create a network of connections between the various rooms and areas. Water becomes the vehicle of change in the building. It designs new spaces, thanks to reflections and lights that originate from neon strips mounted on sections of the suspended volume, giving the impression that the tank contains precious metals. Beneath the tank, stands an area filled with bamboo plants. This precisely ordered, rectangular space filters the light and sends it in a thousand different directions. The alchemy of these elements creates a microclimate which constitutes a perfect example of a bio-climatic architecture. Therefore this building, dedicated to a car manufacturing company that represents and has represented for generations, the reality of a dream, also becomes poetry, magic and dream.

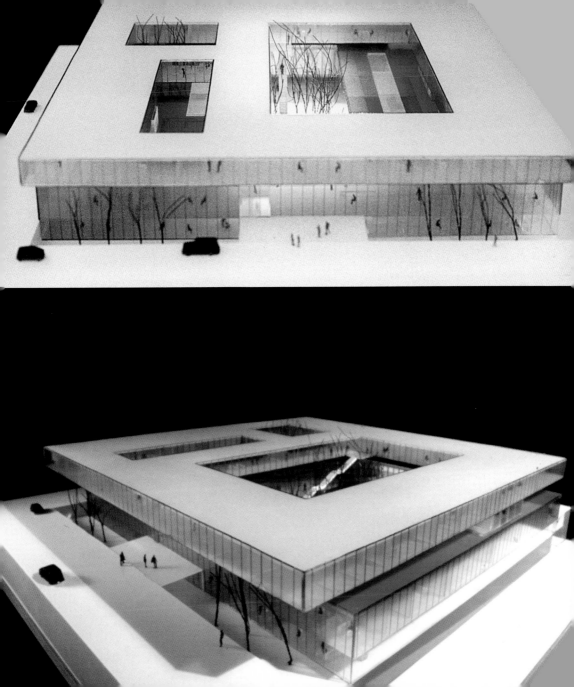

SAN GIACOMO PARISH COMPLEX

Foligno ITALY	2001–2003	**Competition**	**Area** 3 000 sqm

Client Foligno Dioceses	Conferenza Episcopale Italiana

The building consists of two parallelepipeds inserted
one inside the other so as to create three naves.
The first, external structure is made of reinforced
concrete treated with wax, whereas the second is made of
cellular cement and pierced by rays of light from different
sources. The lateral naves are crossed vertically by a
structure that supports the internal box as well as giving
off rays of light that in the poetry of the architecture
become chains. Therefore light is materialized, both
structurally and poetically. The monolithic reinforced
concrete exterior of the building counterbalances the
weightlessness of the interior, which is outlined in light.
Natural and artificial light are further brought together
by the artist Maurizio Nannucci's installation, where
verses from the Bible are written in thin neon lighting.
The church is entered across a bridge and walkway in order
to avoid the use of stairs and to underline the role of
the churchyard. The actual entrance consists of
a vertical cut on one side of the external parallelepiped,
which creates a symbolic split, a point of contact with
the interior.

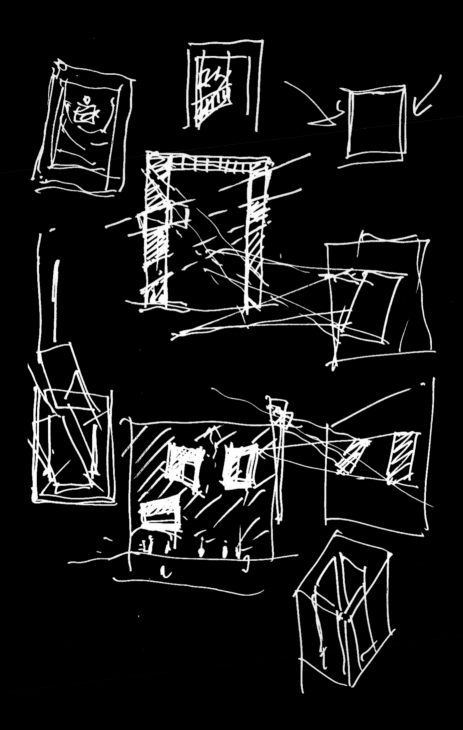

scala 1:500

scala 1:2000

scala 1:200

scala 1:1000

94

1/1/1999

1/1/19

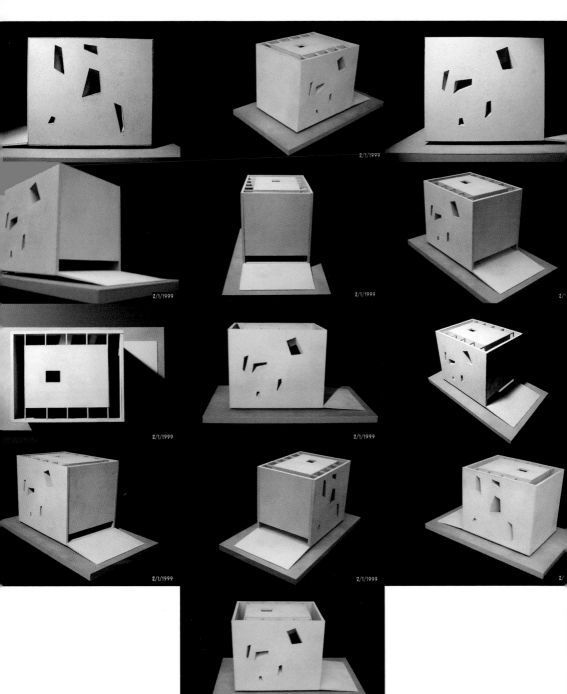

2/1/1999

A homeland for all sailors and a haven for the shipwrecked.
Imagining a place that is not virtual, but real, a place dedicated
to Peace, is an extremely taxing undertaking of profound ethical
intensity. Peace is a spiritual condition, an aspiration, it is
both tension and utopia.
Projecting a will for peace into the future is also an expression
of the hope that our children and future generations will live
in a better world.
Peace, in the sense of a universal value, cannot be closed in a
pre-defined shell, as it represents that sense of fullness and
serenity that a space or a work of architecture can communicate.
I thought of a construction consisting of a series of layers,
a representation of time and patience. The concrete is made of
different sands and dusts that alternate and overlap each other.
The need for a stone base on which to raise the building in
relation to the meeting areas also emerged.
The building is entered from here, by means of two long
staircases. First we enter a place of rest, where the size,
height, and light that comes from above, help us forget
the troubles of the world, and fill us with a positive attitude
towards meeting others.
The outside of the building consists of alternate layers of
concrete and translucent glass. The transparency of the glass
filters the light through to the inside during the day, and
by night sends it back out, entrusting to this magical image the
spiritual and concrete message that the site evokes.
To be effective, architecture must become an "aid", a "hand" to
help us cope with the difficulties of understanding.
This project represents a place in which people can meet and
debate, a place for dialectics and solutions.

PEACE CENTER

Jaffa ISRAEL	1997–2003
Area 5 520 sqm	**Client** Shimon Peres

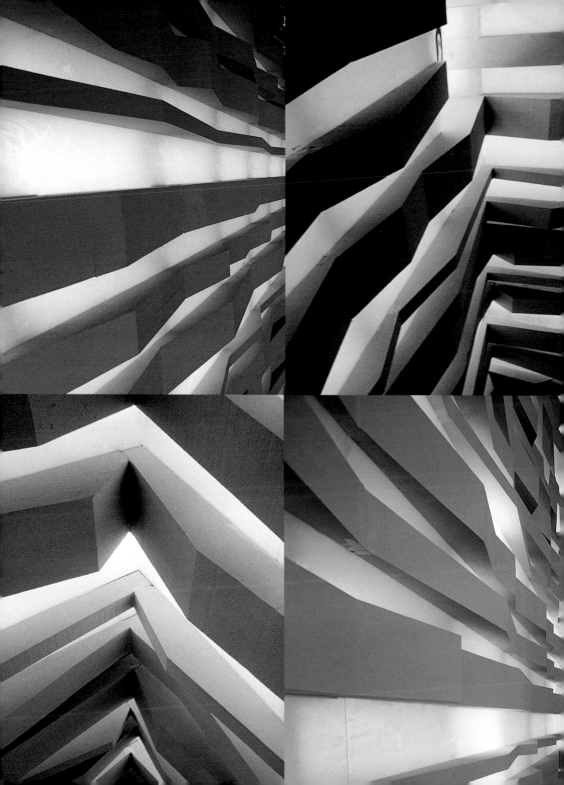

Our main aim is to avoid isolating the site from the
surrounding city. This is why we have designed a space
where cultural activities can mix freely. This is
done by creating rapid connections between the
complex and the city where the major events take
place. Conceptually, our project considers the
creation of three different urban levels,
a residential/office skyline, a cultural belt, and
green spaces for public use. These levels are set
at different heights in order to achieve totally fluid
horizontal circulation.
Another level will also be available underground for
parking spaces and pre-existing structures.
The area is therefore completely permeable, full of
greenery and easily expandable. On one hand, it is
self-sufficient and on the other it has established
new relationships and connections with the city.
The fact that the great park is so near has also
influenced the project significantly. Water winds
into the very heart of the city, creating new leisure
areas. It is an open space that brings most of
the daily pedestrian traffic right into the core
of the city center. It is the "Walking Corridor"
that opens onto the shopping area and passes through
it to reach the pier from where connections are
provided to all parts of the city.

THE SKYLINE One of our priorities is the fact that
the growth of Hong Kong is based on an extremely solid
financial and economic structure.

WATER FRONT RECLAMATION AND REDEVELOPMENT
Hong Kong West CHINA | 2001
International Competition

The possibility of constructing in different phases determines the economic motivation behind every successive action. The skyscrapers do not merely promote the permeability of a project, they also insist on inserting the whole Hong Kong urban experience, as well as increasing interest in the sphere of private investment. The concentration of skyscrapers in a small area creates reciprocal communication at various levels.

CULTURAL AREA   The cultural area is the plan's reference point. It is a compact mass that slips through the conventional rigidity of urban planning formulas. It is the stage on which architecture plays its part by creating special constructions and landmarks. Here we have succeeded in creating a fluid form, pierced in a number of places to clarify and structure the interior space. This whole structure is lifted off the ground and hence remains public space. To create access to the other levels, irregular volumes, that are also part of the structure, intersect the cultural strip.
The circular layout of the holes is used to create a play of light and shadow in the public space underneath.

THE PARK   This is the public entertainment and free-time area. It is vast, free of horizontal boundaries, that transforms the ground into a fluid, not a constructed shape (as in the culture complex) but an absence of construction... a void.

PERFORMANCE SPACE   The large square designed to hold
international events is not located in a far corner
of the area, but rather at the zenith of the project.
It is a location that symbolizes Hong Kong's role as a
major worldwide cultural center. The area is situated
strategically near the museum, as if suggesting that
sometimes the art kept inside may explode. We have also
tried to achieve an open and interactive relationship
between the public spaces and the sea, with the Hong
Kong skyline as a backdrop.

LEISURE CENTER   Situated between the green belts and
the cultural strip, the Leisure Center constitutes the
relaxation area. Set in the center of the complex it
offers access to both the sea and the pier. It is an area
that can be enjoyed during lunch breaks, by visitors to
the cultural centers or by anyone who simply wishes
to take a stroll along the waterfront promenade.

URBAN SQUARE   Surrounded by vegetation and situated
next to the main station, the Urban Center is one of
the points where most of the pedestrians will enter the
complex. Here, the relationship between the cultural
strip and the outside world can be seen immediately.
This is where the life of the city is at its busiest.
Cinemas, theaters, shops and transit systems beat out
the hectic city rhythm that can be lived or watched!
Public events and concerts can be held all over the
complex on temporary stages.

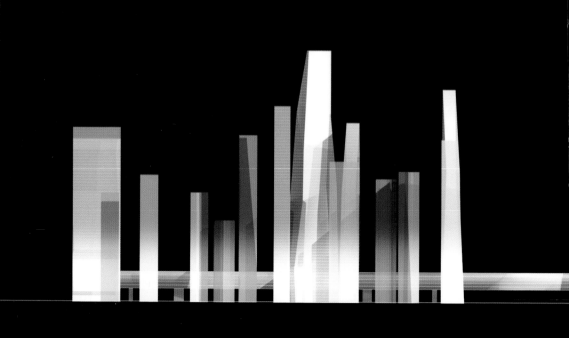

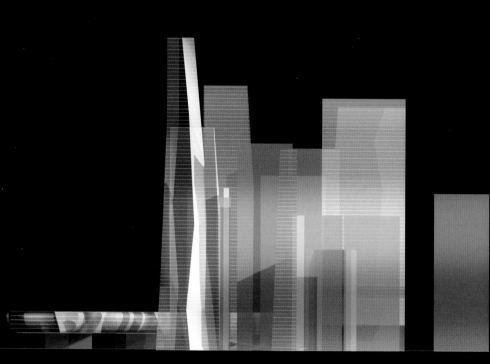

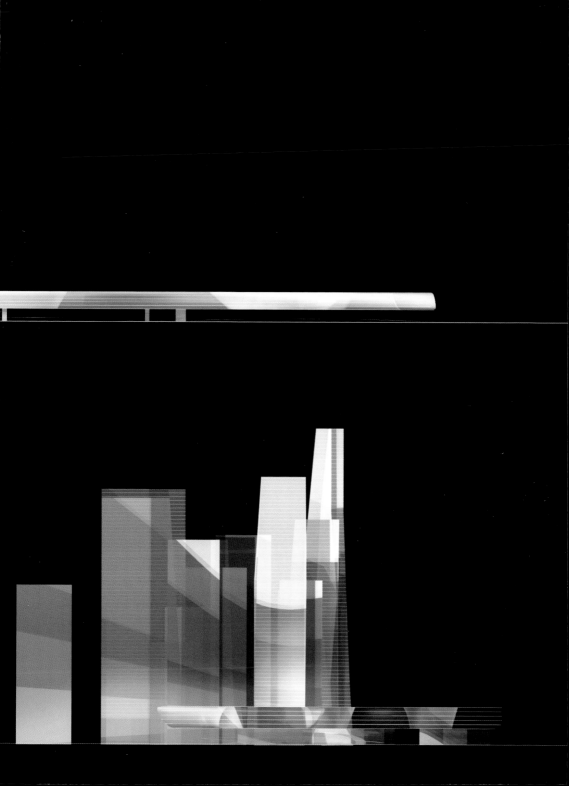

CITTÀ

When the capacity to analyze is lacking for a period
in our history or in our lives, often one is led
to believe that what we are dealing with is a moment
of transition.
In some cases there is nothing to help us understand
the complexity of the phenomena, whereas in others
intuition is simply not enough.
I believe that in the past few years we have been
hurtling through a major upheaval that in terms of
its size and impact is more important than the great
industrial revolution. The speed at which this is
taking place is given by the images that are projected
so quickly that they seem to come from a fast moving
car and days and months are lived in just a few moments.
This all began when Ronald Reagan was President of
the United States of America, and the second phase
of experimental space communication was launched.
The so called star wars were in fact a planetary
satellite cabling system, a digital system that was
becoming a global plan.
The move towards the digital era accelerated at
the end of the eighties. With the Gulf War,
the controls were tuned to the point of readiness as
were the commercial choices both in terms of
space research and new "tools".
Control, command and management, terms that have
always accompanied the myths of power, seem, for the
first time, to be at hand, so much so that they seem
endowed with even more metaphysical connotations.

With the arrival first of the computer age and then
the digital era, the places where control was
exercised, whether out of habit or convenience,
gradually lost importance as centers and subsequently
took on different roles.
I am talking about the city as a physical location
capable of accumulating knowledge and economic growth.
Parallel to the vast change in the planet in terms of
production over the last twenty years, is the constant
growth of the urban population compared to that of
agricultural or rural areas. About three billion people
now live in large urban spaces, or "cities" a term that
has since lost all meaning.
The Gulf War provided an opportunity to test the
efficiency of remote control devices, such as long
distance tracking technology and information systems.
These new tools improved our approach to the nature
of chance and unpredictable events.
Information could be sent and received from anywhere
and in January 1991 satellite information began at
the same time as the conflict started. The CNN
transmitted images of launched missiles and target
hits practically in real time. Everything seemed unreal
and the disaster and brutality seemed almost like
a Star Wars movie. The fear of becoming victims of
terrorist attacks ran so deep in people's minds that
they preferred to stay at home and enjoy the war scenes
live on TV. We were in fact dealing with a strange
"television" war, where air raids, military discussions
and even deaths were transmitted live.

We had definitively opened a new, important chapter
in the history of changes that this planet has had
to undergo throughout its long life.
The loss of the importance of place began to be
understood. During the eighties movement became
faster, distances diminished, possibilities of contact
increased and these innovations began to appear in
movies, literature and in architecture.
First, the internationalization of big cities and then
globalization gradually began to change our tastes and
forms of expression. The exponential growth of tourist
"nomads" was added to regular urban populations.
In the year 2000, France had 56 million inhabitants and
74 million visitors while in the same year, a census
in Italy counted approximately 50 million tourists
and 54 million residents.
Important figures. The great emigration phenomena in
addition to the substantial and continuous changes that
characterize the original nuclei inhabiting western
cities, has generated a system that is precariously
balanced. The "historical" cities no longer look like
their inhabitants. They are no longer inhabited by the
human beings who built them. The memory of how we used
to see them is lost in the fog and speed of change.
A fog that is as dense as the historical urban centers,
as rich as the spaces for the new bourgeoisie, as well
as being wide-reaching and boundaryless for others.
In the city centers the urban lower working class that
has not adapted to the new industrial society has
migrated beyond visible borders and museums, restored

buildings and the uninterrupted flow of tourists or
temporary inhabitants have taken its place.
For at least two centuries the city has been considered
the place of power and control.
The division of social classes was extremely simple:
two warring classes and one to act as a clearing tank,
allowing movement from one to the other to exist in
the collective unconscious.
In the U.S.A. the problem of giving a political meaning
to the changes that have taken place over recent years
is being tackled, but it is difficult for a complex
society to find simple solutions. The places where power
is wielded and the places where it was once centered
are now different.
We must try to forget all this. The city, which for the
best part of the twentieth century was the backdrop for
pain and conflict and which is still full of intense,
complex relationships, has lost its central position.
This centrality comes from the position it held during
the process of western civilization. The incredible,
and in a sense diabolical, clash between the old economy
(cars, arms, petrol, industry) and the new economy,
(communications and control systems) no longer goes
through our cities. These innovations do not belong
to it as they are detached from political parties
and governments. The 200-year-old institutions of
industrial society, which survived great social
conflicts and wars, now appear as faceless leftovers
desperately looking for a new identity in extremely
complex scenarios that know no mediation.

The dream of giving the city back its central position
has failed.
New York used to be the center that accumulated more
people than anywhere else and held more economic power,
but in the 2000 elections the presidential candidates
waited for the results, one in Nashville, Tennessee,
and the other in Houston, Texas. In the meantime in
Los Angeles, in an area of about 170 km x 40 km, lives a
population, the majority of which are Spanish speaking,
whose television hardly ever mentions the city of
Washington, the seat of all government institutions.
It is true then that the city has lost its almost
physical character of power wielder, but these changes
have given it another form.
The struggle that is taking place is between a
traditional economy that is trying to survive these
enormous changes and which, today, is still worth 50%
of production methods (as well as still being part of
our way of life) and an innovative economy that is
no longer in its formative state but is growing rapidly,
enveloping all political parties and definitively
removing any control or prerogative over the future
that they may have. The question concerning the future
of the city that many people ask themselves is, what
form of democracy will we be able to express, given that
we accept that over the next 20 years urban areas will
continue to expand with a rhythm that is at least as
fast as the present one?
What type of city will we live in? ......Cuba is one of the
last countries that still has a vision of a different

pattern of social development, even though it is
full of the contradictions of a period of rapid
acceleration and unlimited consumerism. It has been
preserved, if we can use that expression, by the
American embargo and from destructive tourism.
Havana is at a crossroads, it is on a razor edge and
achieving a balance is very difficult.
35 years after my first trip I find the country
has changed. The enthusiasm of the early sixties and
its impossible utopia no longer exist. The historical
center of Havana, which I remember hazily as being
inhabited by extremely poor people, is now undergoing
restoration. The lengthy restoration work is being
carried out mainly thanks to international aid as the
city of Havana has been declared a world heritage site.
The evaluation of this historical and cultural heritage
is very different from the "Tabula rasa" methods,
typical of modern times, which look to the past with
such diffidence that they simply let things fall apart
or replace them with something new.
Walking along the streets of the "old city" all the
contradictions emerge. The tourist sphere is
relatively well off, while those who remain on the
fringe live in great economical hardship. Despite this
it is each person's dignity that is striking. How long
this embedded sense of belonging can resist the ever
more frequent contact with a very different world for,
remains to be seen. The City built between the twenties
and 1959 is different again. Miramar, for instance,
in addition to its wide, impeccably cared for avenues is

an area which boasts an unimaginable collection of
modern architecture.
German rationalism, mitigated by Caribbean
vivaciousness, the organic unity of composition
typical of 50s Latin-American architectural culture is
only part of the extended concept of "Modern".
This city which has moved its borders beyond the
historical perimeter, the boundary of the corrupt and
joyous pre-revolutionary city, has one of the most
meaningful and sparkling ocean fronts in existence.
Between the brackish foam and the waves that turn
to spray as they hit the artificial rocks of the
Malecón, I can't help thinking what the future might
hold for this land that is suspended in anticipation.
Will it turn into another great megalopolis, attracting
what remains of the rural population, or will
it be the only one on the Latin-American continent
to resist the crisis of a peasant and pseudo-
industrial civilization. The first signs of giving in
are visible. Tourism is the first symptom. Hemingway
and other travelers, lovesick for the "CARIBE" are only
photos in historical locations, "Bodeguita del Medio"
or "Floridita". Cheap hotels with no identity, similar
to many others that have sprung up all over the place
over the last 20 years, to cater for the same old sexual
tourism, families looking for something exotic.
This question, apart from its natural seductiveness,
does not propagate regimental methods or solutions,
it is seeking to identify flexible strategies that are
sensitive to change.

Every time I put pen to paper I seem to end up gathering
together flashbacks and fragments of thoughts from
my trips and constant journeys. Today an architect
is a kind of marble thrown amongst mobile,
non-perpendicular shores that engrave unknown and
unforeseen trajectories.
I believe that each "existence" has traced paths that
are difficult to predict. Despite this, I feel that at
least to a small extent, I am master of my own ways.
This sense of not belonging only subsides for brief
moments, such as a visit to one of my buildings that
expresses its aspirations and what it wants to be much
better than I could, or when I imagine a construction
that fits perfectly with my state of mind.
It is clear that architecture has broken out of its
restrictive boundaries for ever and must investigate
carefully territories and situations such as Cuba,
that are the protagonists of substantial and unexpected
changes. Moments of crisis alternate schizophrenically
with phases of development, following incomprehensible
rules. This is not disorder triggered by social and
economical disasters, but an innovative way of seeking
a new vision of human relationships.
After many years, Havana still keeps its old
seductiveness. The ocean with its sheltered port,
the old city, the 30s and 50s architecture and lastly
the extraordinary era following the revolution in the
early 60s. The true essence of the city, however,
is its poor and modest population, next to whom bars and
hotels, restaurants and shops have multiplied.

WHICH CITY, WHICH LOCATIONS?

The only locations where one can live properly are
those that have not been planned. Clusters of
temporary constructions that grow up spontaneously in
unpredictable places to become locations for meetings
and exchanges. This is the choice taken by people
who live in places that have been planned. It is not
necessary to put the world in order at all costs
or to find a plan that works always and everywhere.
Town planning is not essential, in fact one can say
that the town planner in the traditional sense,
no longer exists and is no longer necessary. We must
grow accustomed to the fact that the familiar
working "context" is now only a series of obstacles and
difficulties. We must contemplate chaos as an
integral part of the urban process. I would even go as
far as to provocatively say, that chaos is the
real order of things and that so-called "order" can
only generate disorder. What I mean by chaos, is
the natural layout of structures as opposed to a
regimental urban plan. The only course of action is
to start at the bottom, from an analysis of existing
conditions, of the spontaneity with which the urban
situation has developed, manifesting its needs, tastes,
attitudes, social contacts and often preserving its
customs and traditions. One needs only to travel from
Rome to Naples, or from Venice to Vicenza, to realize
that not a square meter is still free. The countryside
has disappeared, and been replaced by unauthorized
constructions and disorder, notwithstanding attempts

to tidy things up. The world changes, the number of
human beings increases all the time, and moves from one
country to another according to trends in migration
often caused by political changes.

HOW IS IT POSSIBLE TO PREDICT THESE CHANGES?

How can we accommodate the hundreds of Albanians that
disembark each day along the coast of Calabria,
or the thousands of Poles, Slavs and Romanians that,
because of unstable economic conditions, desert their
country, attracted by a form of consumerism that
they are not accustomed to and do not know how to
take advantage of. They find themselves living or,
rather, surviving on the streets, in any way they can,
which means only rarely working.
The vision of the political party as a mediator has
to be drastically re-dimensioned.
It is also difficult to represent or understand a
contradictory world that uses rapid and complex methods
of communication.
The attempt made by traditional politics to understand
and direct the needs of these new protagonists,
was initially a substantial use of the media.
But the increase in this as well as in low cost Internet
technology and digital platforms has reduced the
effect and power of communication and persuasion
using established methods.
A different method was then tried and "market research"
was adopted to understand the complexity, needs and
requirements of the changing society.

The city became a test zone, a research center.
If at first, the theory on which this research was based
gave some good results, as time passed the complete
fragmentation of the system had a contradictory effect,
making the results totally worthless.
The speed at which our system is breaking up has reached
a point at which it is impossible to keep up with the
fragmented and pulverized needs, interests and desires
of today's society.
Unpredictably, but with a subtle logic, urban areas
develop independently and anarchically. Ten years
ago no one would have thought that Rome, with its
800 thousand motorcycles, could become like Bangkok,
or that the desperate and difficult to manage outer
fringes of the greater European urban areas could
ever be compared with the cities of south-east Asia,
in terms of subsistence levels and production
processes. Numbers are no longer the form but the
substance of urban development and this must
be accepted before the changes in cultures and new
inhabitants can be analyzed.
Life is to be found beyond the 12 km diameter of
the "Ville de Paris", beyond Amsterdam.
In the Hague in Rotterdam what was once known
in Holland as countryside is now a huge suburb of
single family houses.
A highway ring connects the three big cities.
Every hour of the day vehicles wind their way along
this outer ring road, in both directions, at an
exasperatingly slow pace.

London persists with its own principles of modernity. After years of calls for a return to the past, which were fortunately unsuccessful, the city has undergone massive changes, completing an old planning project begun in the early 1960s.

What we are witnessing is a desire to modernize that is so frantic it leaves us speechless.

These are megalopolises where boundaries are lost in a regional dimension and London finds itself experimenting not only with the integration of populations from the old empire but also with a new wave of immigration from Eastern Europe.

In Asia, in addition to Hong Kong, Shanghai and Peking, hundreds of satellite cities are growing at an uncontrollable rate. The speed at which this is happening has swallowed up the complex order of cities with unexpected fury.

It was thought that underdeveloped areas would follow exactly the same growth pattern as that of the western world which took centuries to develop.

Culture and digital technology, allow even extremely dangerous areas to move directly from an underdeveloped state to a highly advanced economy, in much less time and using minimal resources.

In a recent trip to India, I visited a number of very different regions. In Delhi, Bombay, the new city of Chandigar and in the tourist center of Jaipur, I realized that the role of the university as an agent of economic growth and general development was the real added value factor. In fact, if a city has a pole of educational excellence, it immediately takes on a role, it becomes a "place" and its growth and magnetism turns populations and cultures, that are different but also united and standardized thanks to this new technology, into experimental areas.

The economy is no longer based on quantities produced but on the brains behind the production and innovation processes.

Over recent years, mankind has invented tools that can be compared with the breakthroughs that became known as the industrial revolution.

The fabrication of "invisible means" does not fill cities with monuments, nor does it celebrate the new economy with spectacular towers, impressive complexes or any concrete manifestation of strength and economical power. The structures it creates are invisible and the methods used are a refined, almost alchemical production of artificial intelligence such as communication and information systems.

Urban areas are celibate now, or rather they are widows of the great Van der Bilt or Rockefeller myths, the families that built Manhattan.

Nowadays, for cities and architects the client is invisible. This is what we have to face up to.

The accumulation of resources is revealed through the world of "funds". It is as if life has become too long to present us with anything certain.

This anxiety is the insecurity that comes from crossing undefined boundaries and it reproduces the myth of eternity in unaccustomed ways. Religion alone can no

longer explain the logic of existence. Age and health
are only marginal factors of life. Even funerals or the
sending off of the dead no longer interest the city.
They are concluded as rapidly as possible and replaced
with births like products that have expired.
The beginning and the end, the places we belong to have
been forgotten and erased from memory.
Groups or forces that have been defeated and pushed back
in the face of these great changes move threateningly.
Nevertheless I am convinced that everything is radical
enough to sweep aside any trace of "nostalgia".
Calcutta or Dakka, the two cities that attract the
greater part of the entire population of Bangladesh,
or Kuala Lumpur (one with a regional urban area of
approximately 44 million human beings, the other with
at least 14 million inhabitants) are examples not
only of extreme growth rates but also of development
and production processes. Calcutta is a case of
spontaneous development that does not adhere to any
civil plan, whereas Kuala Lumpur, a city which is
growing at an incredible rate, has seen neighbourhoods
grow up in response to the fact that movement has
become impossible. The loss of public control means
that every individual activity has to integrate a
number of factors. In other words, the Megalopolis
has become a modern form of nomadic existence.
Clusters move and change continually in a ductile
context. This is why the Megalopolis has little or
nothing to do with the metropolis. The metropolis
does not experience these problems and, in turn,

the Megalopolis often does not even have a center
and is therefore not polycentric like a metropolis
Tokyo is a Megalopolis that somehow works because
it is a city that has developed without a plan
or program. Tokyo has developed on two structural
levels instinctively. On one hand, there are
the skyscrapers, and business buildings, in other
words a vertical and often multifunctional evolution
where on one floor there may be a museum and on
another residential apartments. On the other hand
there are the conventional, old low-rise houses
and traditional restaurants.
Tokyo did not explode after instinctively adopting
this twin development process (of vertical and
horizontal), it actually improved. In this case the
complexity of a Megalopolis was resolved without
anyone providing a "cure" or having to adopt a plan
or create rules to organize the unorganizable.
It is even more interesting than New York, which,
even if it represents the prototype of the modern
city in the collective unconscious has now become only
another historic city, where modernity
circulates without difficulty. Unfortunately after
the events of 11 September 2001 everything is now
cause for debate.
Communication, data and control systems are no
longer sufficient for a population that moves faster
than information.
The complexity of the Megalopolis is also the reason
for its existence.

Typology no longer exists, it is a concept that is
no longer valid, as a form of common emotion is what
is needed.
The city is a city that is extendable, that expands and
contracts enormously. The new city no longer
has predefined routes, it is a city in chaos, which
does not mean disorder but sublime order.
Powerful elements of organization and accumulation
are born from this situation, and commerce, culture,
and museums become one and the same, places that are
almost a simulated copy of the city, of another city.
The possibilities of finding work or other advantages
demonstrate without any doubt that suburban areas,
far away from the main residential centers are hardly
developing at all.
The incredible rate of development of new
communication systems has definitively given birth to
individual enterprise, to molecular enterprise.
Individuality and fragmental groups or associations,
represent a new society that cannot be segmented
or disassociated and which is motivated only by
specific group interests.

Excerpt from "Caos Sublime". Massimiliano Fuksas with Paolo Conti.
Milan 2001, Rizzoli

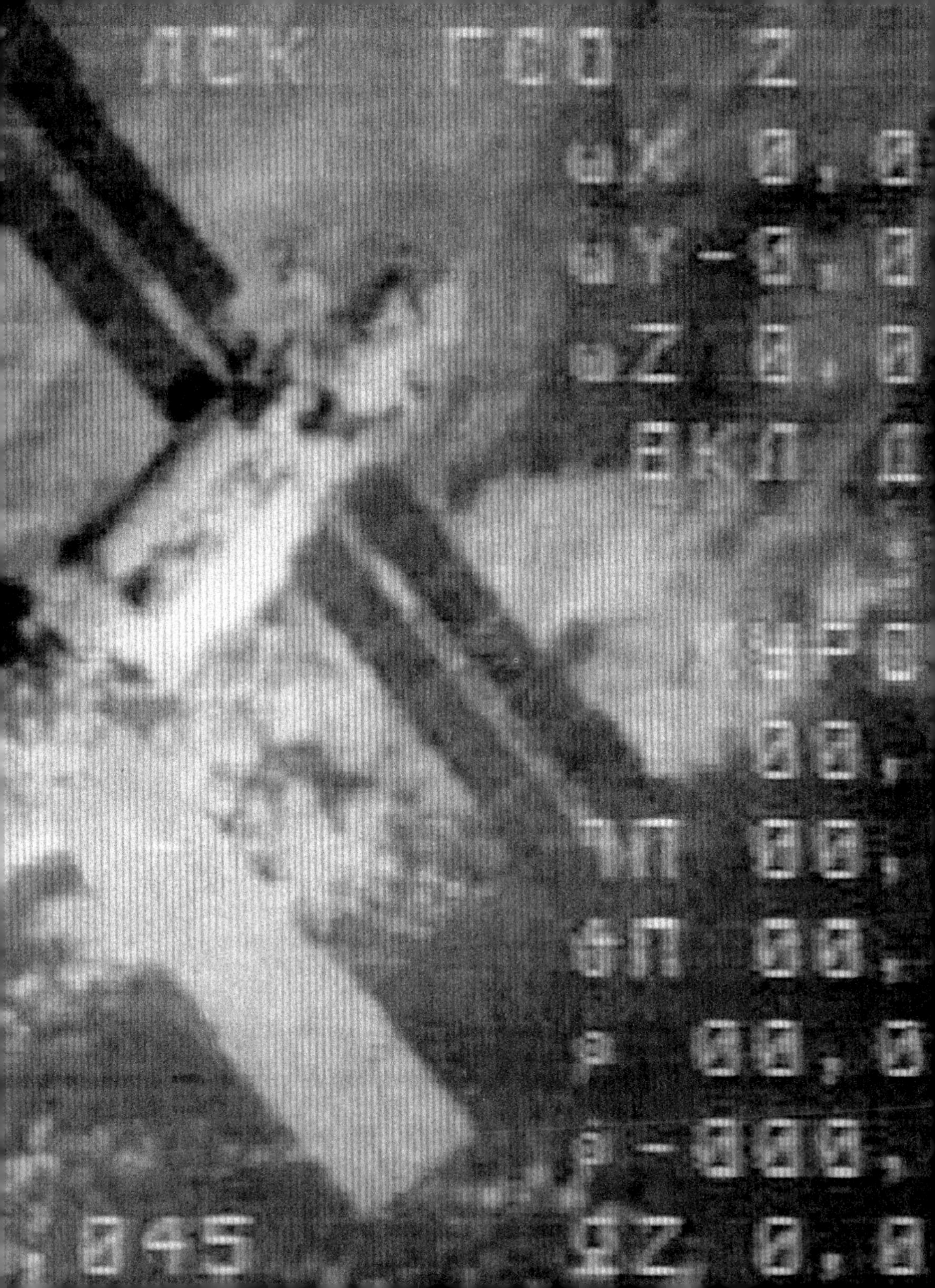
045

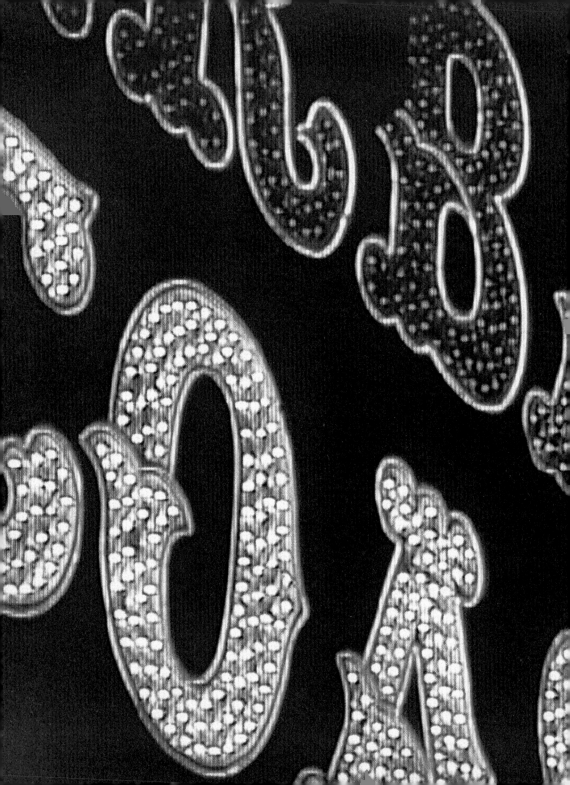

7th Biennale di architettura di Venezia 2000
CITTA': LESS AESTHETICS, MORE ETHICS

Cities and their contradictions explain why millions of human
beings prefer to be "stockpiled" within a small, malodorous
area, in tiny, expensive apartments, surrounded by all
manner of dangers. The city evades all rules. We could try
to endlessly classify and simplify it, to try to discover
the magic. But, it is a diabolical magic and any attempt at
classification would prove to be banal and out-of-date.
It would seem that once the city has overcome its various
growing crises, it becomes an infernal machine that cannot
be controlled in any way. At this point, it can bear any
form of intervention because its consistency and structure
have become formidably strong. It can withstand errors and
wounds by simply absorbing them and getting used to living
together with any form of devilry, no matter how difficult,
is part for the course.
Let us abandon the city made of buildings and look rather
at its streets, squares and no-man's lands; at the things
that nobody wants to use.
It is in these above ground arteries and below ground veins
that the energy of the city flows. Its sap and nourishment
are the cars and the thousands of human beings that crowd
together, all of them trying, in an infernal puzzle,
to find the right street, address, cinema, meeting place,
job, money etc.
If, just for a moment, we could take away all the buildings and
look only at the people, the famous city people, the people
we meet in the lift or on the escalator, on the bus or in
the subway, it would be like watching some fantastic show,
and we couldn't help but wonder where all this great mass of

people are going, what ant-like instinct they are imitating, and, above all, why.

There is no point in wondering though. The alchemy is complete and we cannot go back. We can analyze it in terms of voids, which I think is the best solution, or in terms of spaces that have been filled, which is definitely worse. But then again, both voids, voids that have been filled and even the enormous tensions that create and release energy cannot explain the urban phenomenon.

Once we have established that no rule exists and that no rule is needed, the city becomes a complete abstraction. Just look at the way tall buildings alternate, the way low buildings and towers alternate, and yet all of these live together simultaneously.

A tree every so often has a greater value than any tree in the world, as it is lost in the great concrete jungle. In spring, these trees have such presence that they can make a road pleasant by emphasizing its irregularities.

I think of that while the plane is landing in Shanghai. Everything has to start again. The hotel, perhaps the only colonial style hotel still standing, is in Bund. Bund is the Shanghai equivalent of the Riverside in London or Hamburg. This place is legendary. It appears in both films and books. A city front on the bank of a river. On the other side, approximately one kilometer away (the distance separating the two banks), stands a city that has become a megalopolis in less than ten years. It has spread beyond all belief without anyone trying to control it. Towers spring up before your very eyes.

The crowd is crazy, the contradictions are enormous.

The most amazing thing about Shanghai, about Peking,

is the speed at which the process of transformation is taking place.

New cities spring up and before you know it they can already hold up to 20 million inhabitants. This situation has never been seen before. They are cities that are developing without any architectural culture whatsoever.

We have been flying over the Île de France for ten minutes now waiting to land.

It is night-time and the city and surrounding landscape below us looks like an enormous vibrant spider's web.

Cars, houses and highways come together to form a fabric of flux, tension and energy.

Energy and tension, the differences in potential between a "weak" area and a strong one are not enough. Perhaps there is something magical, some tremendous alchemy that transforms matter and fills it with dreams and invisible emotions.

VISIBLE... INVISIBLE.

And if the relationship between the visible and the invisible were at the root of this urban, this life-giving, alchemy? Invisible paths, invisible to those who cannot see them, hold Australia in a tight-knit web made of "invisible" monuments, representing the nomadic era when the aborigines moved from one end of the continent to the other, "leaving poems and songs, right and left, as they went". And each one of them, at birth, was entrusted with a "song" and the place it corresponded to.

The language used now is the same language, created through poetry, not writing. Is not this what we need today? This way of creating the future by inheriting a portion of "collective spirituality" from Poetry? Is not satisfying oneself with

only the pragmatic relationships, the relationships that
indubitably emerge from cities, simply a way of becoming lost
in another mad attempt to make rational what is irrational?
The city is a place of despair and excitement, of opulence
and homelessness. But the city hides a heart in its depths.
Listen to your heart, city!
Beuys said that art has to become "aid". What he meant by
that is that art today, in addition to ¡aesthetic¡ pleasure,
minimalist graphics, the tactile matter of plain art or
the fury of abstract expressionism and action painting, must
play a "helping" role in letting the "involuntary creator"
emerge in all of us.
We come across this unknown artist in the street. He is the
one who must recognize and take care of the fragments of
poetry that already exist or that will exist in the future.
He is the one who does not kill for pleasure, who is
tolerant and respectful, who tracks down the invisible and
communicates the magic of existence to others who, will,
in turn, communicate it to those who come after them.
Everyone dreams of a city in the same way as they dream
of life and when they do so, they imagine what is best,
what is perfect. The space that corresponds to a dream is
therefore possible but we must continue to feed it with our
imagination. We must continue to speak about the metropolis,
and not the city, about the dreams of millions of people
that nourish urban monsters, about the changes in places
and spatial functions.
Above all, though, it is our duty to act in cities. Our war
aims to improve life and its resources, to demolish the old
disasters and to replace them with a new dimension that gives
humanity to life and life to mankind.

CITTÀ: LESS AESTHETICS MORE ETHICS

Director Massimiliano Fuksas | **Video Installation** 284m x 5m

written and directed by Massimiliano Fuksas & Doriana O. Mandrelli

The large videowall (280m x 5), which we installed on the occasion of the 7th Venice Architecture Biennial Exhibition, is dedicated to megalopolises. It tries to find a scale of intervention that, after the utopias and the beginnings of the Modern Movement, no longer belongs to us. We made films in eleven megalopolises and one of the things that emerged was the duality of values and the total ambiguity. A city can present itself as a classic, tourist, picturesque, ethnic or cultured stereotype. On the other hand it can show its contradictions, its cruelty or the marginalization in which, every day millions of human beings live their lives. Unfortunately, many of the situations that we filmed turned out to be a lot more serious than we had expected. We touched on some of our planet's most delicate problems, such as pollution, the destruction of forests, desertification, the nuclear risk ... We have tried to provoke an emotion, but more than anything else we have tried to make people think. No one is interested anymore in self-referential architecture that spends all its time looking backwards. We all live on a borderline that is continually crossed and violated. The undulating motion that can be used to summarize our way of moving forward has two constants, curiosity and information from distant worlds. At present, we are leaving a critical, perhaps even privileged, position, outside the "magma" of infinite relationships and interferences, to navigate and move in an unknown "discipline", full of energy and contradictions. Its minimal forward movements are also ours, in fact we are responisible for them.

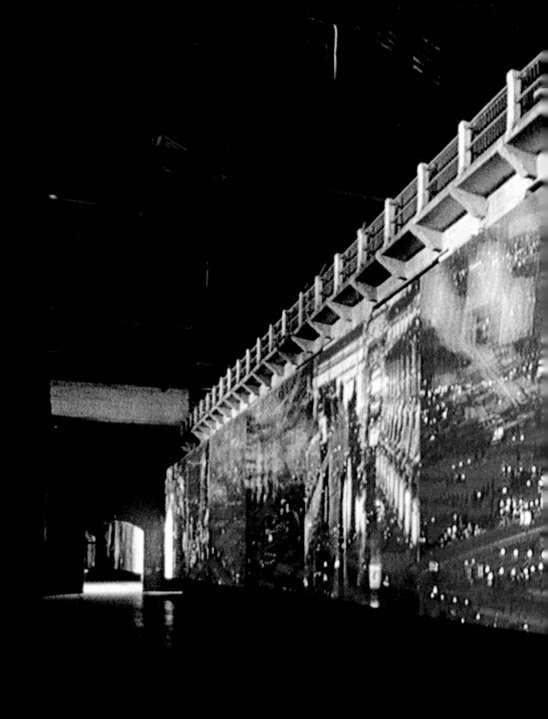

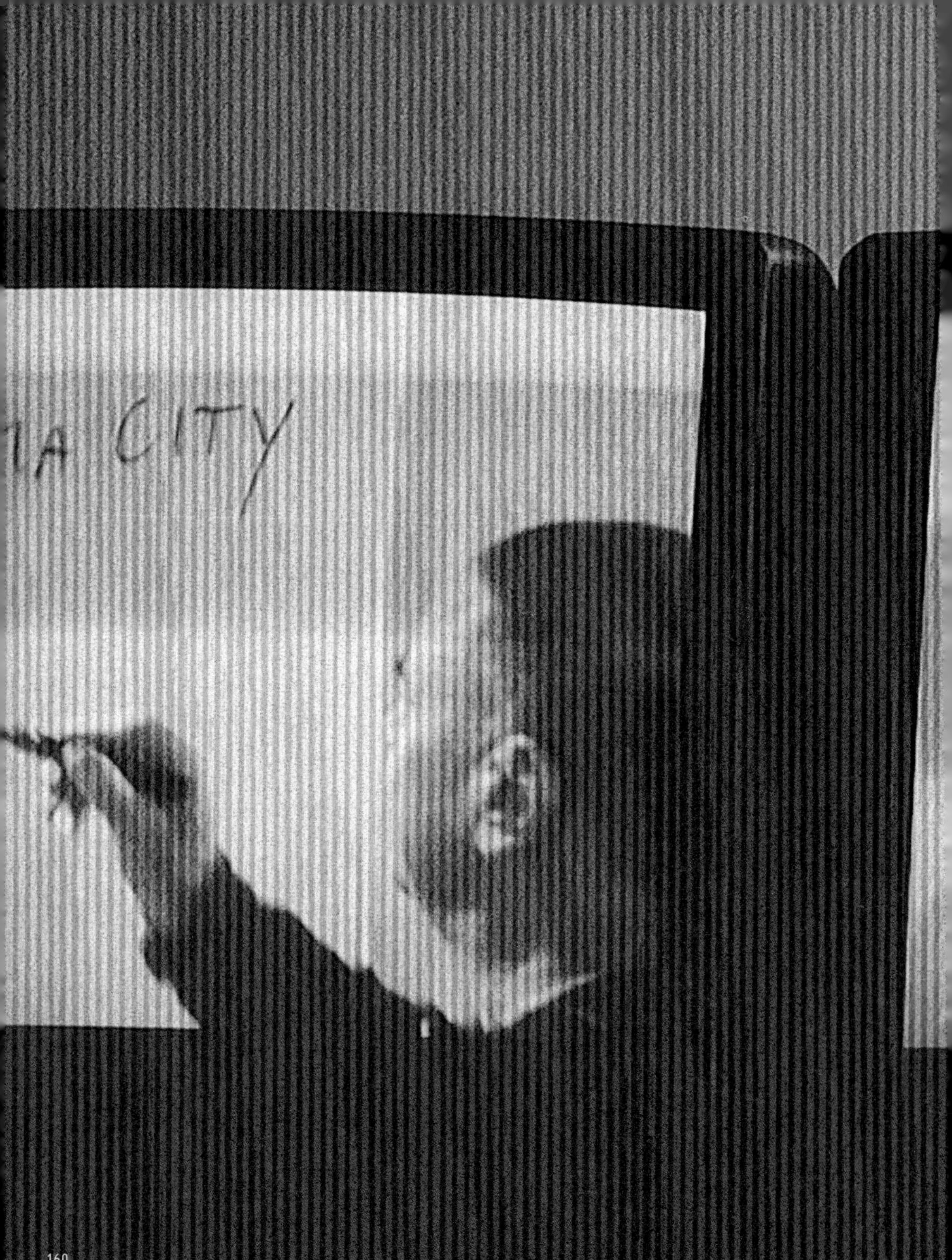
IA CITY

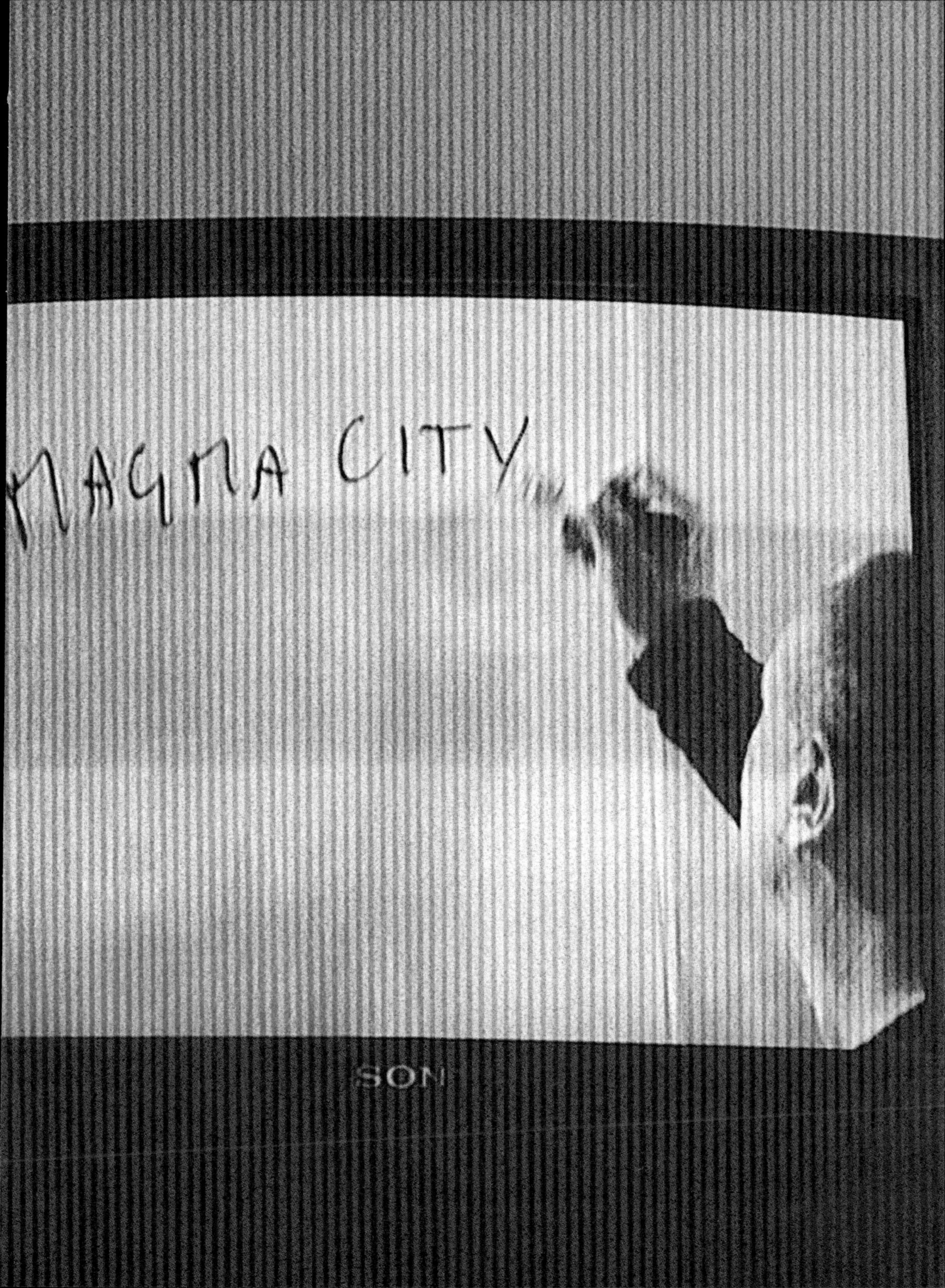
MAGMA CITY
SON

MAGMA CITY

centro consolidato

nuovi luoghi

1. traiettorie sconosciute
2. algoritmo non conosciuto
   ~~Affutura~~
3. CAOS = NUOVO ORDINE .
4. geometria variabile -
5. reticolo = impresa di singoli ind.
6. collegamenti privati (~~tanto~~) -

MAGMA

It is my firm belief that architecture is capable of
giving a new image to the urban landscape, and this
is why I never speak of scale, because scale
is related to the human being. An object or a
building are big because we are small and viceversa.
The horizon is far more interesting because it
is dynamic, because we rise or fall with what we
look at. It moves together with us, and this is a
completely different way of looking at things.
I never use the term "landscape", as I prefer the
word geography. This is because I believe that this
concept includes landscape, economy and human
beings. It contains a form of organization that is
not a mere outline. Geography is much more.
I think that a good architect should be a
geographer. I always try to give energy and
tension to my projects. Perhaps if we start from
this premise we can we really start to change
things. What else can we do! We have built
everywhere so we can build somewhere else, but it
is hard. What is our future? Yes, we have built
a lot. We have fabricated a landscape that is
strange and at times interesting but, most of the
time it is dull. We spoke of suburbs right through
the 80's. But once that has been proved, what are

we to do? We can start demolishing, but we can also
start to transform, to change, instead of simply
destroying. Often the only way to keep a building
alive is to change its function, to adapt it to
meet new requirements. We have to bear in mind that
contemporary architecture will last less and less
and that if a building or project already had a
limited existence, now it will last even less.
Due to the constant urbanization of this planet,
the economic value of a manufactured product and its
construction loses its importance and is replaced
by the assessment of areas, especially central urban
areas, which are the most valuable.
In my opinion, we are at the start of a fantastic
century. However we run the risk of turning it into
a worse disaster than what went before. On the other
hand if we use the means we have at hand, we can
move in a completely new direction, and leave behind
forever the typical, post-structuralist attitude
that is still anxious to "tidy things up".
The city is like a constantly evolving shape that has
no limits or borders. It resembles a MAGMA where
differences and origins come together in a state
of permanent conflict.
If it were not for their size, we could think in terms
of districts, of the past conflict between different

urban neighbourhoods, of quarters and communities faced with new migrations and invasions of urban territory. Place d'Italie in Paris, is populated for the most part by Chinese or, better, by Asians; Little Italy in New York has been taken over by the Chinese community; and an enormous area in Berlin is populated by the Turkish community.

Cities are the worst place to live in, but they are the home of the economy, of exchanges, the place where one can get rich. They are a continuous and exciting contradiction.

When I think of a contemporary city, what comes to mind is an uncontrolled archipelago of irregular buildings. If you put something rigid and geometric among them, you will interrupt their spontaneous rhythm. Instead of order, the only result will be a new disorder. All this in the name of an ideal model. The average modern individual, living in a rich city, is usually organized as an individual firm. He or she moves by car, reaching other individual clients and following the tension that his or her business transmits. This creates a completely new universe, but unfortunately, the means we use to move around are archaic. Cars and planes burn highly pollutant fuels that alter the ecological equilibrium irreversibly.

Only a real development in technology, which
I believe is still at an early stage, can change
such a situation. When it is possible to organize
our lives in real time using Internet, then we
can start thinking about a new society and new
architecture. The use of computers, the love for
virtual architecture and "liquid" and "amorphous
masses", as well as a different system of graphic
representation can lead naturally to a strange
organic/virtual architecture. It almost seems that
this type of architecture disassembles and then
reproduces, down to the smallest detail, the
molecular structure of life. Man is no longer
displayed in terms of his external appearance,
it is his living mechanism that is analyzed and
investigated. Virtuality has an extremely positive
influence on the architects' work. Thanks to
Internet, we no longer need to move in order to
send or receive information in real time. It is very
useful for students, for example. They do not have
to listen only to their teachers anymore as they
can visit all the major architectural studios and
widen their horizons. The only risk we run is that
at the end of the day the so-called "style" may
become standardized, which is something I have
always rejected. What is true today may be different

tomorrow and certainly nothing looks like it did
yesterday. Working in uncertainty, in areas that
have never been explored before, is something that
I find indispensable. I do not agree with people
who repeat the same project, the same outline, year
after year, even if this makes it easier for them to
become famous and recognizable, given that a "style"
is certainly far more reassuring than eclecticism.
As far as I am concerned, working in a space that has
not yet been defined, that has yet to be created,
that has no obstacles to take into account, is
almost unthinkable. On the few occasions that
I have experienced this, I felt lost. Difficulties
and contradictions are the rule, in my book.
If they are not there, I almost have to create them
so I can work properly, so I can operate within
a chaos. This proves that urban development plans
do nothing more than slow down the process of
adaptation. In the same way that walls are useless,
and only exist to be knocked down, like in Berlin,
with the ultimate wall.
The idea of "ordering disorder" often only makes
the existing situation worse.

Excerpt from "Caos Sublime". Massimiliano Fuksas with Paolo Conti.
Milan 2001, Rizzoli

Funsc@pe can be described in three key-words: integration, landscape and flexibility. The name funsc@pe encapsulates three different concepts that are all in harmony with each other, fun, information (@) and "landscape", and are all directed at the visitor. Shopping is certainly entertaining, especially if it is integrated with a series of activities from the world of leisure and relaxation and that is what takes place here. The project gives great importance to the mediaplex, intended as both an architectural space (a multimedia plaza with giant screens and web-cams connected to all parts of the world) and an information center. The center is conceived as an artificial landscape where visitors can move fluidly between the various levels in total relaxation. The whole funsc@pe center is conceived as a unique organism that integrates space and vision and creates an innovatory landscape of entertainment, information and shopping. The roof and the +549.0 level change shape alternately. They grow in height and depth when they reach certain attractions (for example the free-climbing demonstration wall, the mediaplex, the giant swimming-pool slide and the Baumarkt garden-center). The contraction-expansion of these two fundamental elements creates surprising and continuously changing viewpoints and adds greater flexibility to the spaces involved, not only at a two-dimensional, but also at a three-dimensional level.

BERN—MALL AND ENTERTAINMENT CENTER

Bruennen SWITZERLAND	2000
International Competition Project award winner	
Area 95 000 sqm	Client Genossenshaft Migros Aare

The Mall, the heart of the center, has not been crystallized in defined, irreversible forms or surfaces, so it can be expanded, if necessary, in the future. The Mall is conceived as a "progressive" structure that can readily take on new shapes and forms and adapt to the changing movements and behavior of both visitors and retailers. The project is carefully inserted in the wider Brünnen context and takes into account the construction of a residential quarter in the immediate vicinity. A clear visual link has also been made between this area and the town center thanks to the canopy which starts as an opaque color and becomes gradually transparent, thus allowing the vertical structures containing the entertainment areas to be seen. The project is in complete harmony with the concept of green areas for public use and the plan includes one to the east of the complex and one to the west of the forest. The green belt to the east (situated above the highway) which crosses the park has been placed at the point where the residential quarter meets the funsc@pe center at the 554.00 level, and mingles gradually with the Mall.
The language of the funsc@pe is both a communication tool and a way of constructing a new identity for Migros and the city of Bern.

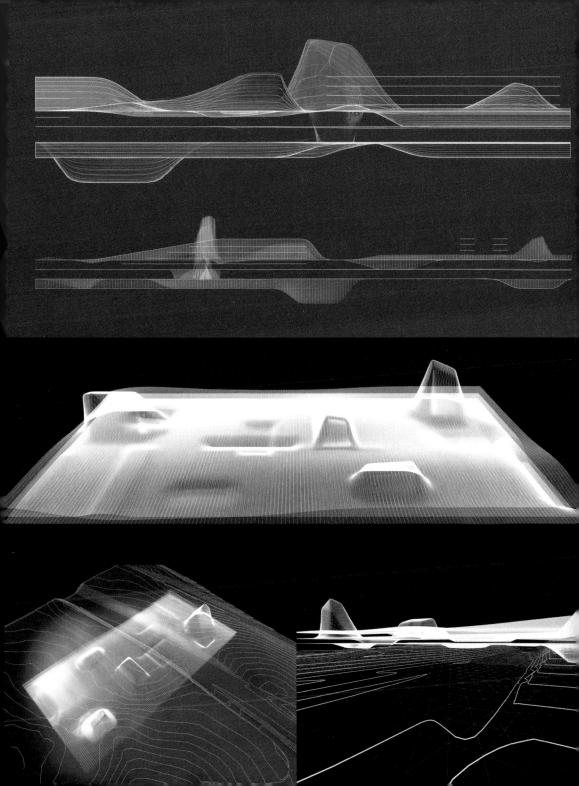

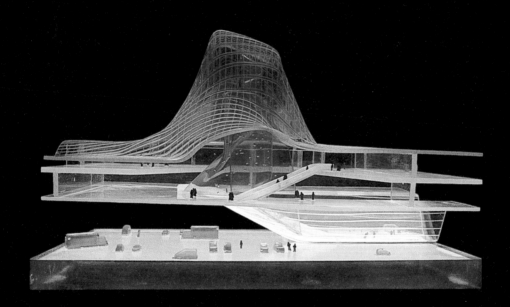

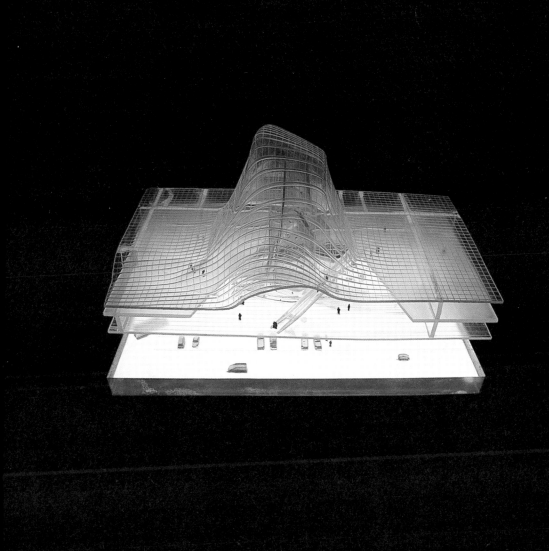

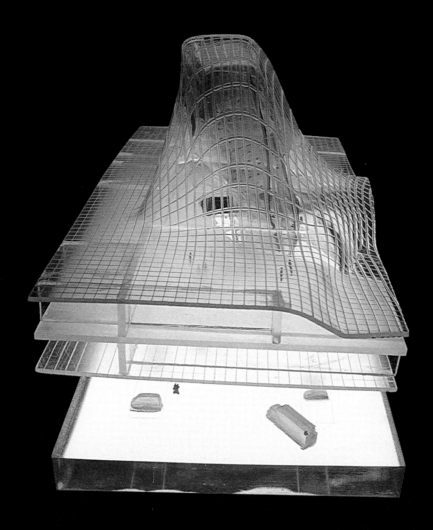

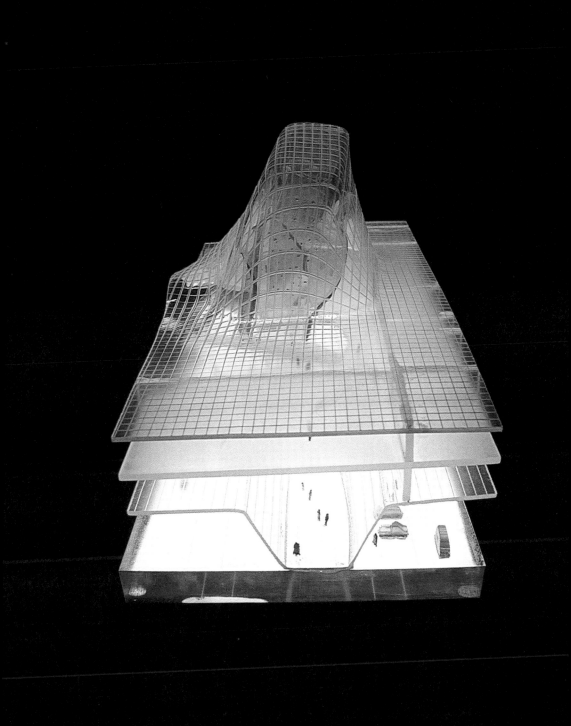

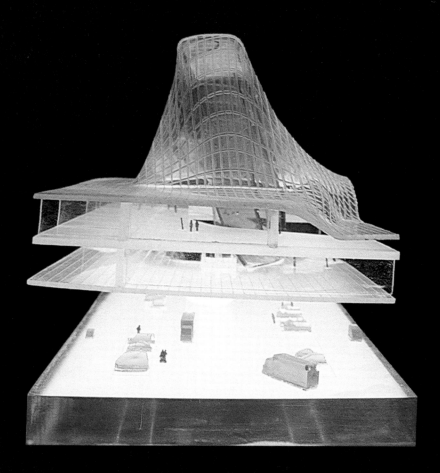

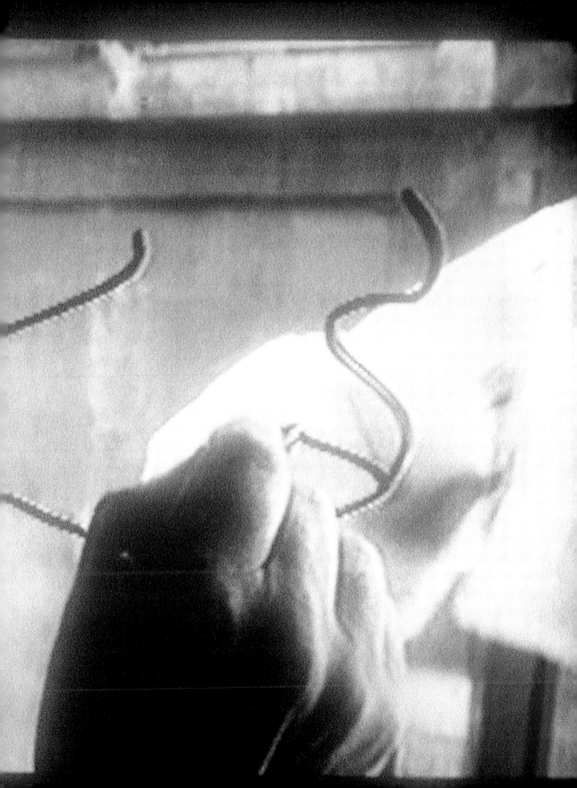

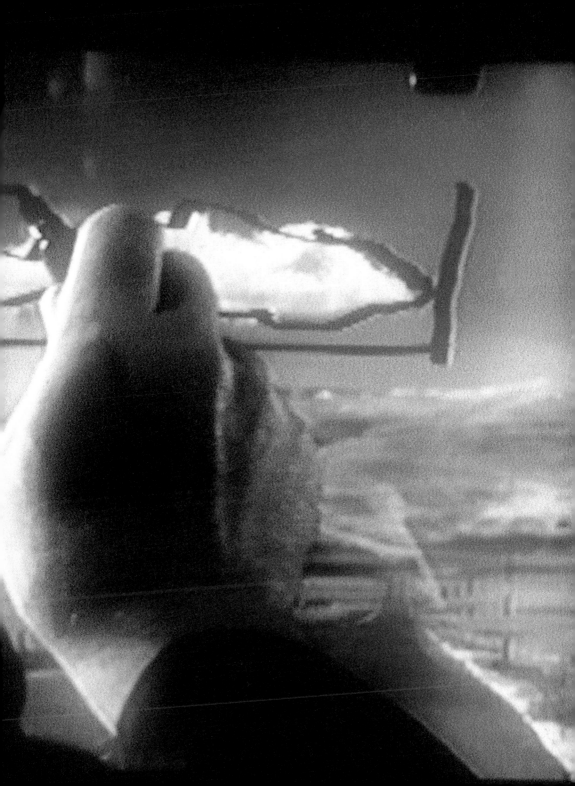

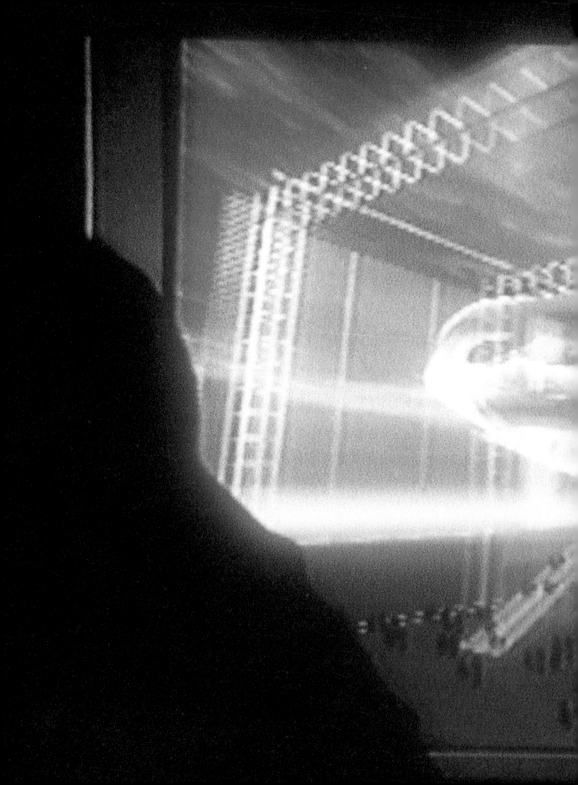

ADVERTISING and ARCHITECTURE   Stefano Casciani

Fact and fiction were definitively short-circuited with the
arrival of the new millennium. The much-feared Apocalypse,
the "End of the Real World" has, at least for now, been consolidated
by its fusion with the imaginary. The hundred painful versions
of "Big Brother" and above all the painful destruction of the Twin
Towers are painful precisely for reasons which are both opposite
but convergent. The former because they *pretend* to be real without
actually being so, the latter because it *resembles* fiction but
is not. This is only the latest version of a Hollywood movie.
Cruel beyond all limits, needlessly bloody and almost unthinkable,
but for this very reason real, it has already been dreamed up by
scriptwriters and watched by audiences time and time again.
This was just another reconstruction with a few insignificant
changes made by mad religious fanatics who are no different from
their counterpart *wasps*. In this complete confusion, art, the only
thing which can really make the world despair and go insane, is at
the same time an accomplice and a route to salvation.

It is an accomplice because for at least a hundred years it has preached what is happening today. It represents salvation because in its authentic form it also indicates the possible alternatives, like the puzzles in popular magazines, which have the solution (upside down) at the bottom of the page. What are the solutions to the false Real/Imaginary dilemma put forward by the art of Massimiliano Fuksas, even in his latest "advertising" persona for Renault? People can imagine new versions of reality as a positive reaction to their own madness. Whether this relates to buildings or advertisements is of relative importance. When a certain "alternative" television critic speaks *of and on behalf of* a generation which grew up with "Carosello" (the forerunner of Italian TV advertising) they are not simply making a witty remark. Instead they are describing, with ironic brevity, an objective condition, which only echoes that of other generations, such as that of Venturi and Gehry, who were brought up on Walt Disney and his characters, or that of Rem Koolhaas, raised on Archigram and Batman. So Fuksas's return to advertising aphorisms (which in a single digital gesture summarizes the entire struggle that moved Italian architecture towards real, contemporary post-modernism) becomes the best and most efficient advertisement for many subjects and discussions as well as for pages and pages of magazines, articles, essays, books, videos and exhibitions – from "his" Venice Biennale project onwards. Fuksas can be provocative, mocking, contradictory and wild in his designs, but the industry, which saw his unforgettable R4 become one of the symbols of the '68 Cultural Revolution, could not have chosen a more appropriate figure to personify the reasons, effects and hopes of another Revolution: the Digital one. The only revolution that has both problems and solutions for a world which is not willing to simply accept its disappearance into the as yet unsolved Real = Virtual equation.

CONGRESS CENTER "ITALIA" EUR

Rome Italy	1999-2004	International Competition

Area 26 981 sqm	**Client** EUR s. p. a.

"The idea came to me in a very special moment. I was at the seaside and a group of clouds were being blown quickly across the sky by a strong wind. As I looked at the clouds I remembered a dream I had had, which involved constructing a building that had no crystallized form at all." The building is basically a large, 30 meter high, translucent container that extends lengthways. On each side a square opens onto the immediate area and the city. The first converses directly and continuously with the local area and can be crossed from Viale Europa to viale Shakespeare. The second, a space that can be composed freely using moveable structures, is for welcoming conference participants and accompanying them to the various rooms in the center. The simple, squared lines pay tribute to the 1930s rationalist architecture that characterizes so strongly the EUR and the nearby Conference Center designed by Adalberto Libera. Inside this shell, a 3,500 sqm steel and teflon cloud is suspended above a surface area of 10,000 sqm, designed to hold a 2,000 sqm auditorium and various meeting rooms. In addition the center will also contain three halls and spacious foyer, café and restaurant areas, covering a total multi-functional space of 15,000 sqm. When the cloud, supported by a thick network of steel cables and suspended between the floor and the ceiling of the main conference hall, is lit up, the building seems to vibrate. The construction also changes completely depending on the viewpoint of the observer.

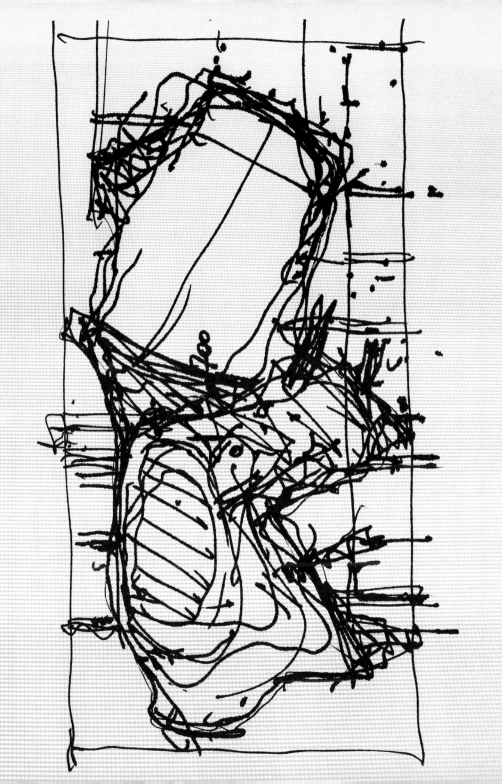

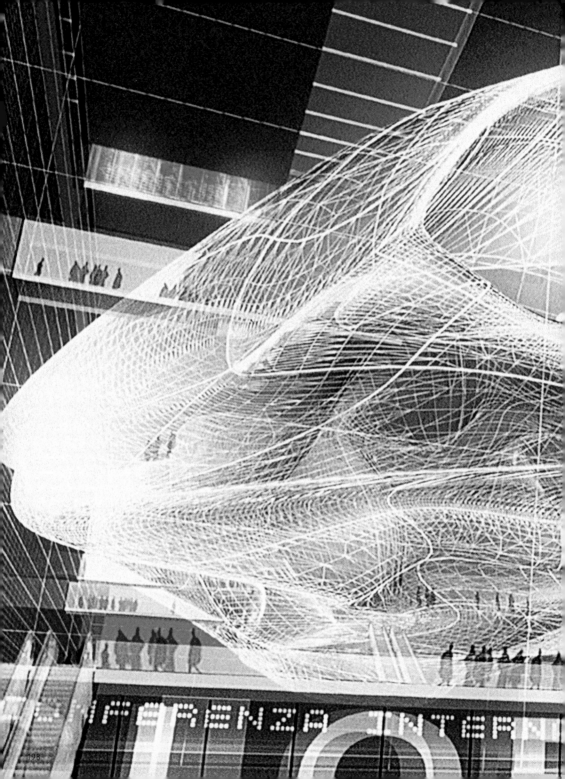

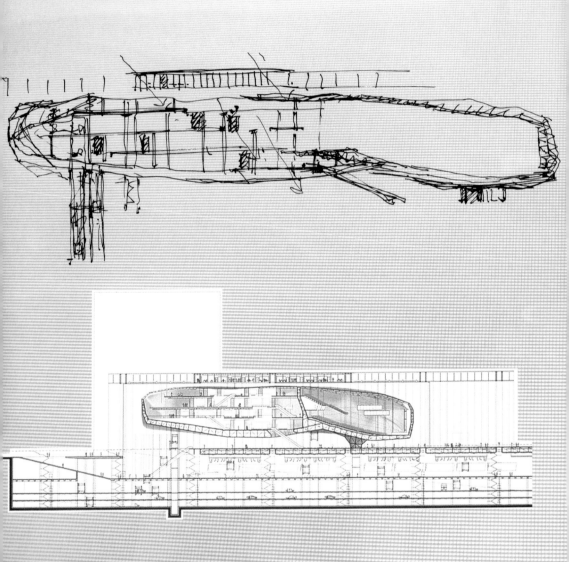

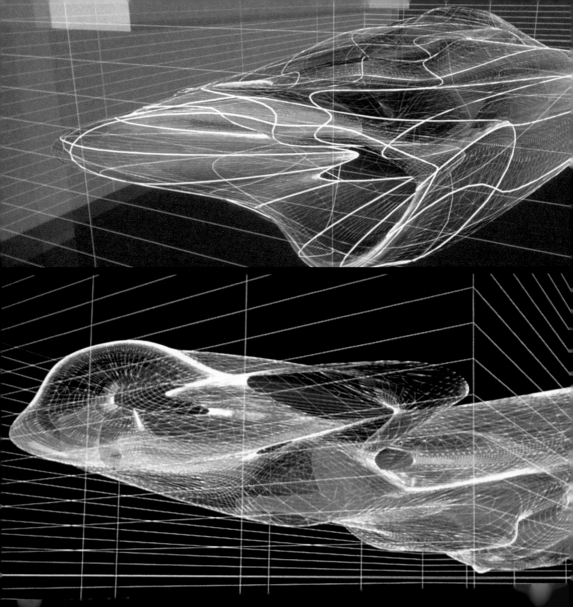

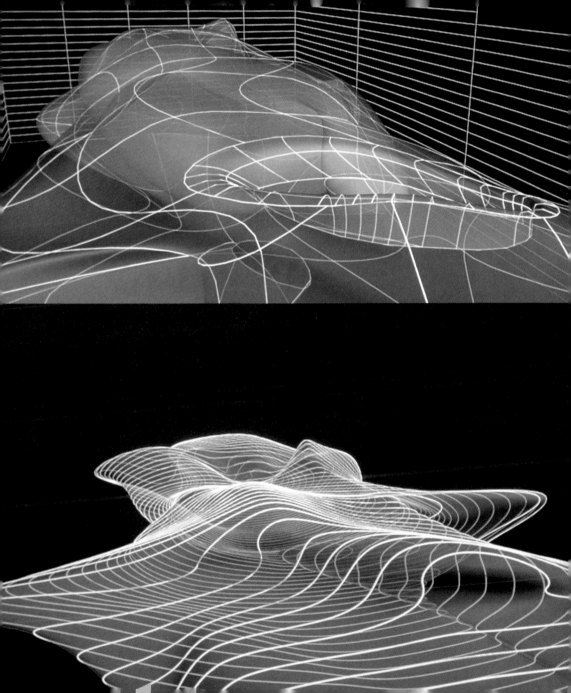

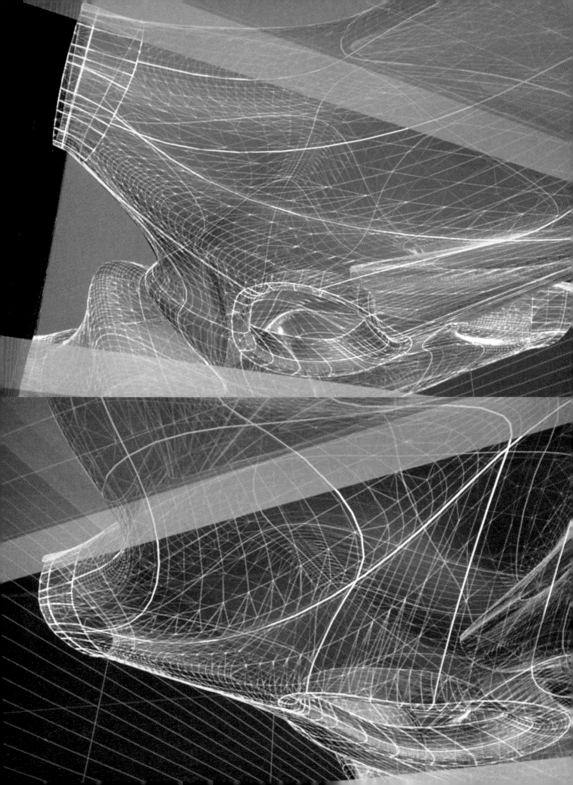

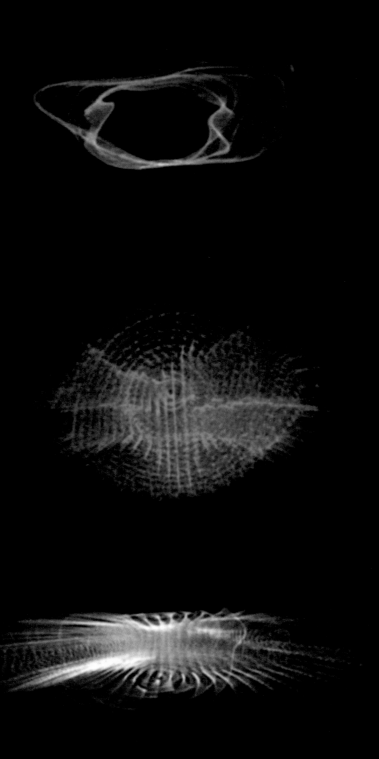

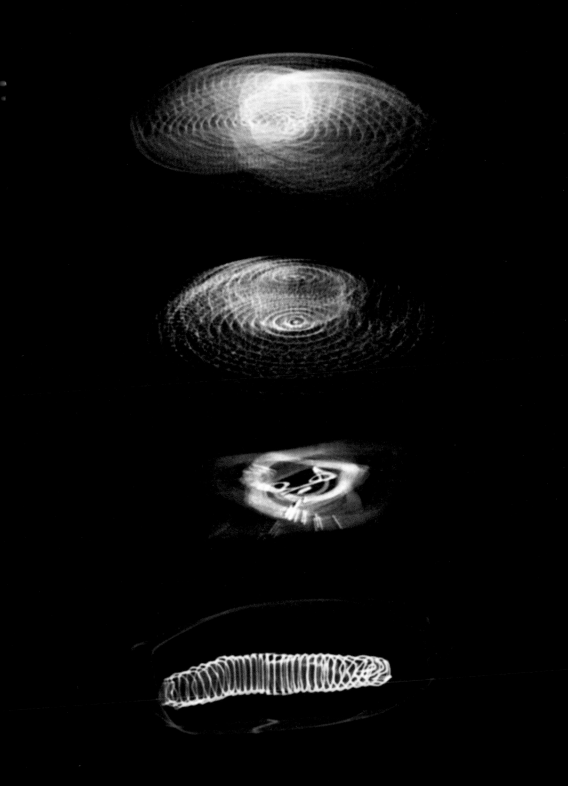

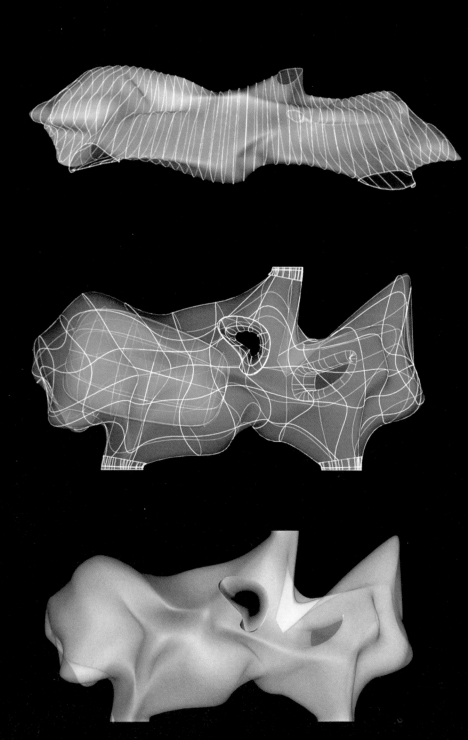

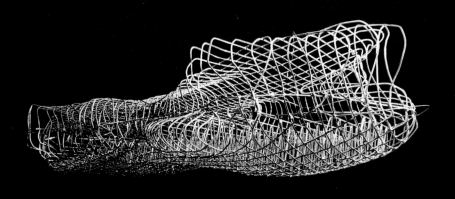

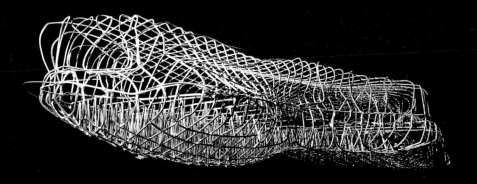

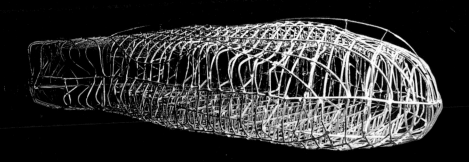

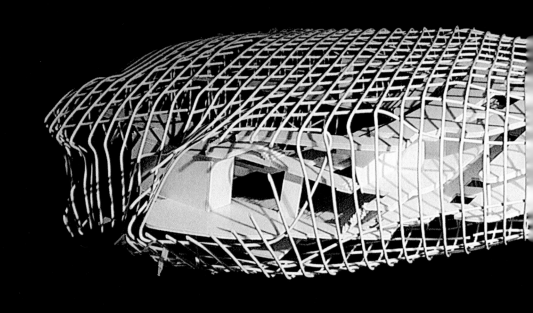
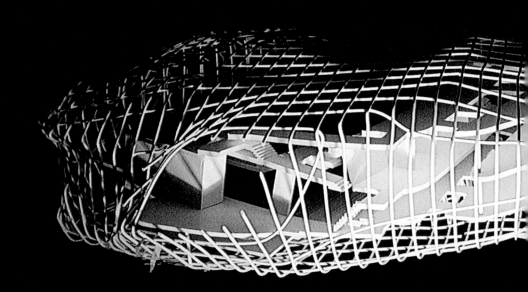

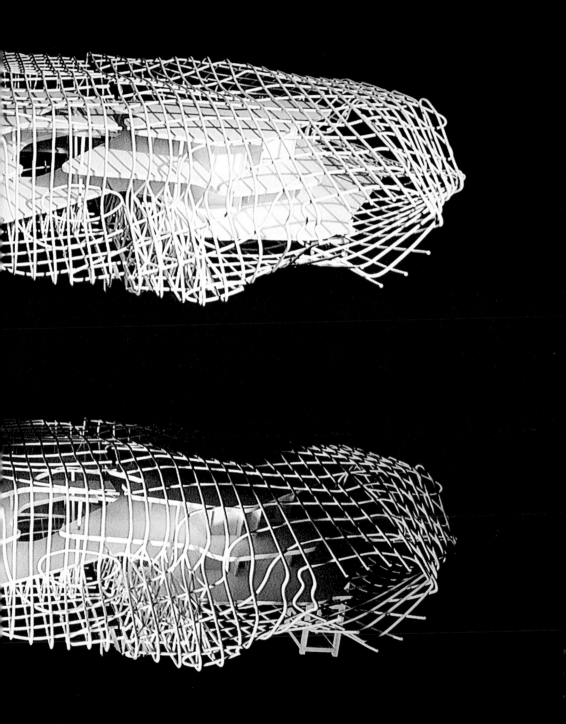

NEW ITALIAN SPACE AGENCY HEADQUARTERS

ASI Space Museum and Multimedia Center

| Rome ITALY | 2000–2003 | International Competition |
| Area 6 000 sqm | Client Italian Space Agency-ASI |

The building, in keeping with the existing ones,
extends lengthwise, as can be easily seen from via
Masaccio and via Guido Reni. In deliberate contrast
to the architecture of the neighboring church,
the building is surrounded by a spacious green
belt which forms a visual connection between the
two streets and constitutes a communicative link
between the new ASI building and the Zaha Hadid
Contemporary Arts Center.
The structural layout consists of three functional
strips, arranged in such a way as to distinguish
staff areas from those for visitors and those open
to the public. The first strip stretches out towards
via Flaminia. It is a fixed band and contains the
offices for the President, the Management,
the administration and all the organizational
support units for the various Agency sectors.
It is based on a simple structure consisting of a
distributive band, where the size of the rooms can
be modified, thanks to the mobile wall panels.
The second strip forms the core of the building and
is the most flexible one. It contains the facility
blocks and the distribution structures, which are
fixed by definition. It is, however, designed in
such a way as to allow the expansion of areas from
the third strip. The third strip welcomes the flow
of visitors from the entrance in via Masaccio.

It is conceived as a fluid space, with no co-ordinates, where two continuous bands mark out concave and convex areas assigned to the multimedia room, the cafeteria and the exhibition area. The hall on the ground floor becomes the distribution point for the flow of visitors into the building. It is also the starting point for the museum itinerary which proceeds to the upper floors, illustrating the evolution of scientific space research through a display of models, satellite prototypes, space stations, launching pads and films. The cafeteria, open to both ASI staff and visitors, is situated just above the multimedia room and is connected directly with the hall.

The multimedia room can be reached directly from both the hall and the exhibition itinerary and is equipped for conferences and public presentations. An opaque/transparent/translucent liquid crystal screen counterbalances the rigid, horizontal tectonics of the Contemporary Arts Center. With its liquid crystal screen, transparent surface and curtain wall, this constitutes the real interface between the building and the city. The new ASI building can therefore "participate" in the city while at the same time becoming an urban landmark, communicating its own character to the outside world.

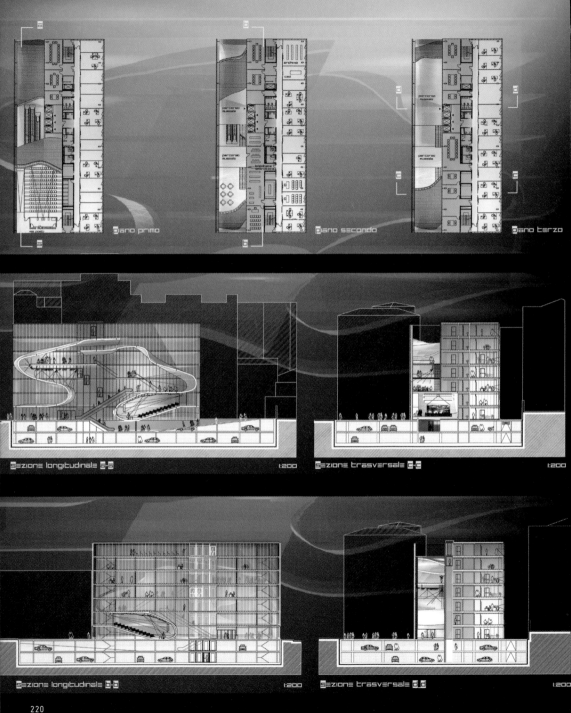

piano primo

piano secondo

piano terzo

Sezione longitudinale B-B   1:200

Sezione trasversale C-C   1:200

Sezione longitudinale A-A   1:200

Sezione trasversale D-D   1:200

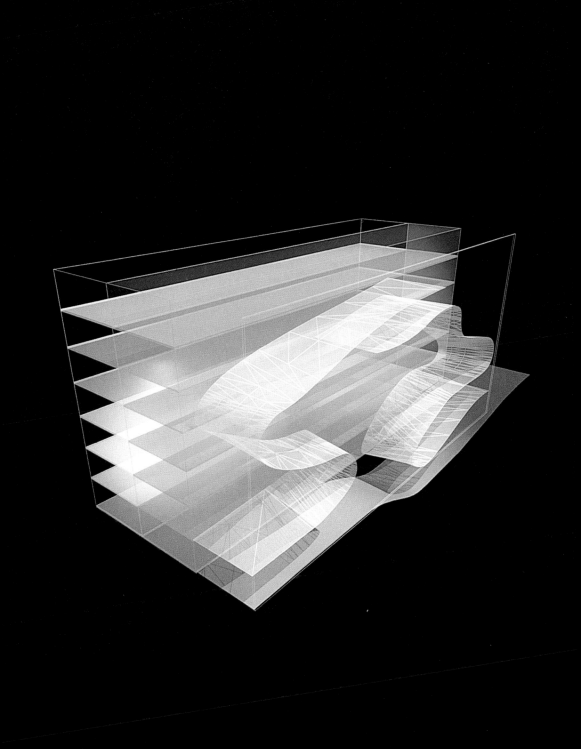

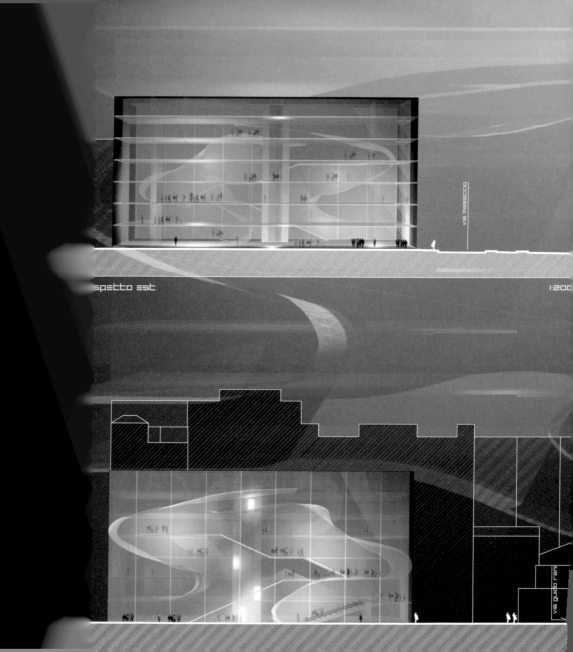

spetto est   1:200

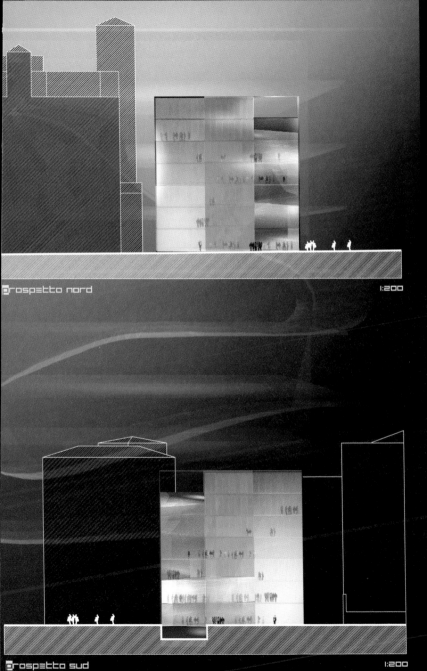

prospetto nord   1:200

prospetto sud   1:200

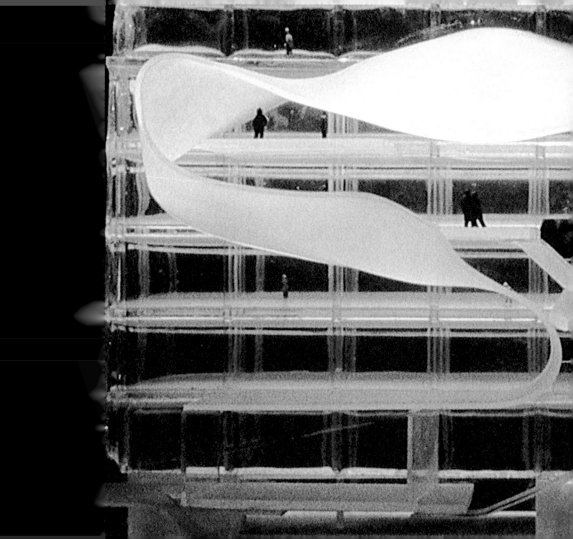

This symbolic building that is recognizable without being
isolated is also the central element in a vast and complex
system. The project for the new Headquarters of the Piedmont
Regional Council creates a dialogue not only with the adjacent
buildings but also with its whole regional context. The building
is balanced in relation to the local territory by adhering to
the cardinal points and establishing a relationship with the
surrounding natural elements: the mountains, the plains,
the river, and the hills. It is a landmark on the Turin skyline,
a powerful element that can be identified immediately.
Despite its representative and corporate value, the construction
also succeeds in interacting with the environment at both a
spatial and functional level.
This project is part of a proposal to redevelop the area based
on modifications to its backbone axis. Although the building is
aligned perfectly with the axis, it also allows it to interpret
its role freely and thanks to a variety of different functions,
it becomes a catalyst at all hours of the day and night.
The complex consists of two elements: the tower in which the
Regional Council offices are located and a lower building
containing the Conference Center and other services that the
city can take advantage of.
The interface between the two is the "great void" or knife edge
that represents the unifying space of the entire complex.
This functions as an entrance hall to the offices and Conference
Center on the bottom floors and on the top ones it provides
represention areas for the region.
This space may be monumental but it is also transparent and
permeable. It is a live filter through which the building opens
out to the city and the city enters and becomes a fundamental
part of the building.

NEW PIEDMONT REGIONAL COUNCIL HEADQUARTERS

Offices, Exhibition Center, Auditorium		
Turin ITALY	2001–2004	**International Competition**
Total Area 35 000 sqm	**Client** Piedmont regional council	

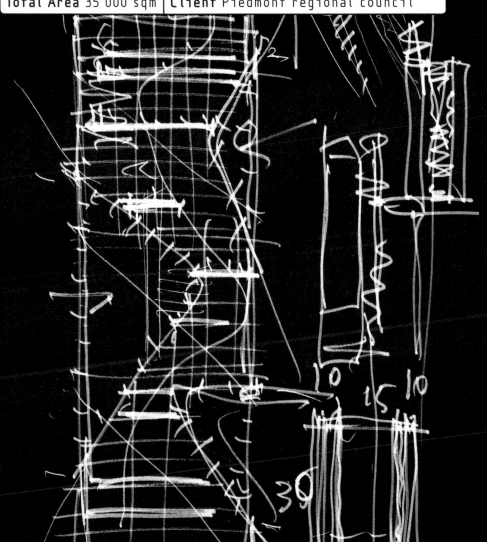

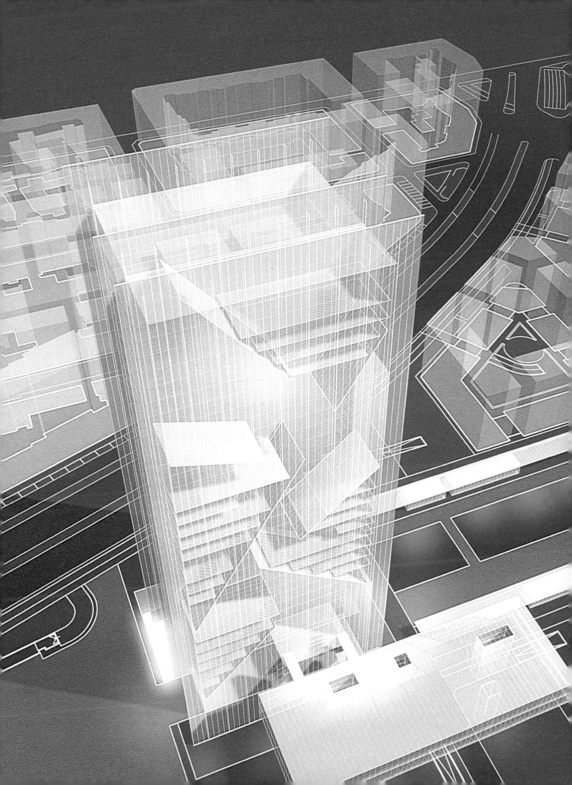

sezione a–a' scala 1:200

PIANTA PIANO TERRA (0.00)

PIANTA PIANO SECONDO (+6.80)

INGRESSO PRINCIPALE

STADIUM

Wals—Siezenheim, Salzburg AUSTRIA	1999

International Competition Project Award Winner

32 000 seats	**Client** SWS Wals—Siezenheim

The new concept that this project is based on
is the construction of a membrane that surrounds
the stadium ring.
This membrane is a neutral environment that does
not belong to either the local geography or
architecture. This project surpasses even the
concept of landscape, be it natural or artificial
(as determined by the architecture).
The building is an element that exists naturally
and in harmony with its local context and only
stands out on account of its unique form.

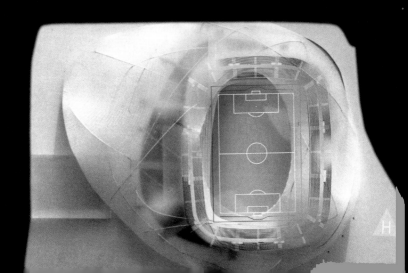

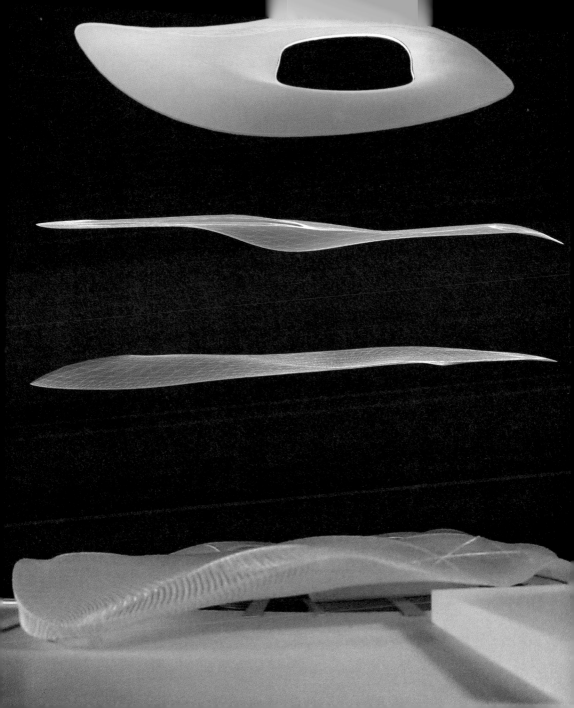

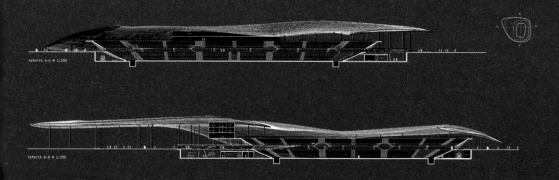

schnitt A-A M 1:200

schnitt B-B M 1:200

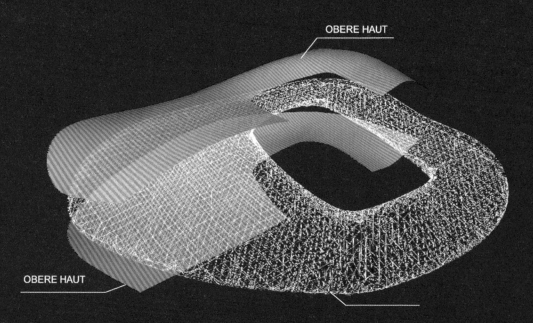

OBERE HAUT

OBERE HAUT

TRAGWERK

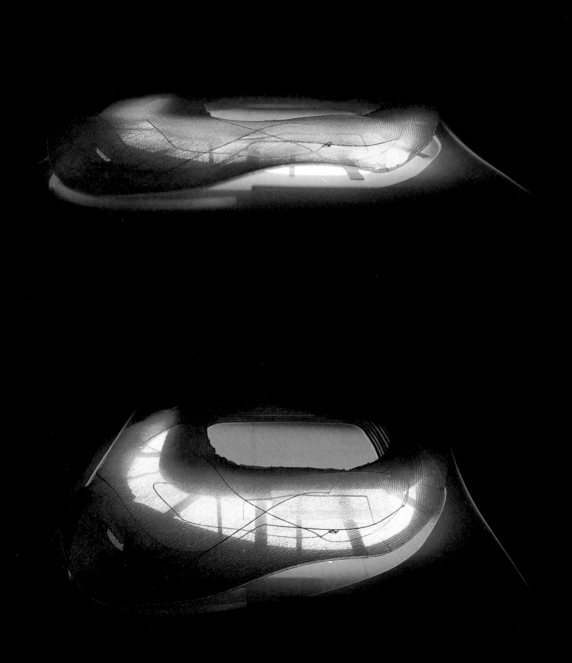

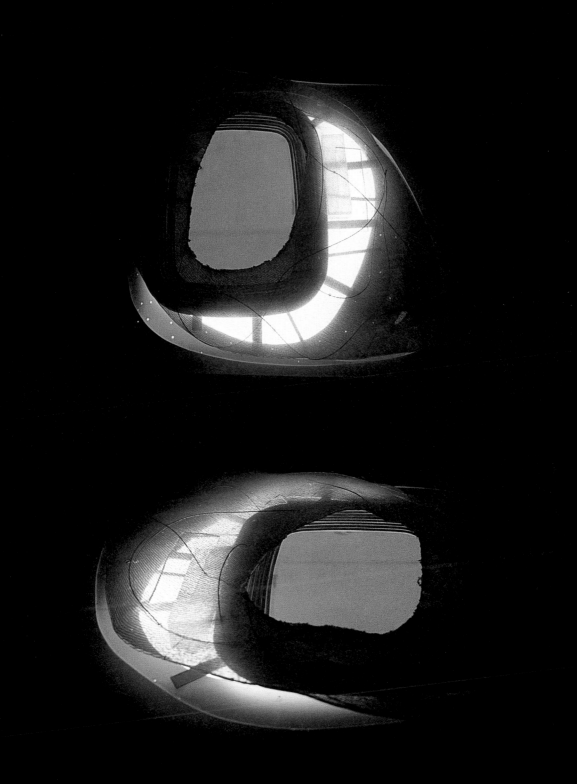

This project involves plans for a new district on the site previously known as the "Herzo Base" in the town of Herzogenaurach.

The "World of Sports" building is situated on the east-west axis inside an ecological forest ring separating the complex from the residential and industrial parts of the town.

The Adidas "World of Sports" building will be a new focal point for the town. In line with its innovative design, it contains various activities under one roof, including offices, laboratories for researching new materials, residential areas and, of course, multi-purpose sports fields and facilities. The canopy covering the structure, can be either timber or glass depending on the activities that are taking place underneath it, and has been designed to create a spacious foyer, overlooking the entire complex. The vegetation has also been chosen for both aesthetic and functional reasons. One important use being to create various separate areas for different sports events.

A number of different sports facilities are situated in the forest ring itself. These include football and baseball pitches and a golf course laid out around the natural greenery. The far side of the forest ring will house the new residential and industrial zones.

Residential zone The houses are located in harmony with the natural topography of the area, and they too are oriented along the east/west axis in order to take full advantage of the sun.
The interiors are designed with the same principle in mind.
Home layout plans have been made extremely flexible to satisfy a wide range of social needs. A vast number of home types make various solutions possible, including single and family apartments as well as specially designed housing for the elderly or handicapped.

Commercial area The commercial area will act as a buffer between the Herzo-Base and the city of Herzogenaurach. The structure can be extended in all directions to integrate with the various parts of the town. The area can also be expanded internally to integrate existing businesses and to attract new ones.

ADIDAS WORLD OF SPORTS

| Herzogenaurach GERMANY | 1999 |
| International Competition Project award winner |
| Area 62 000 sqm | Client Adidas |

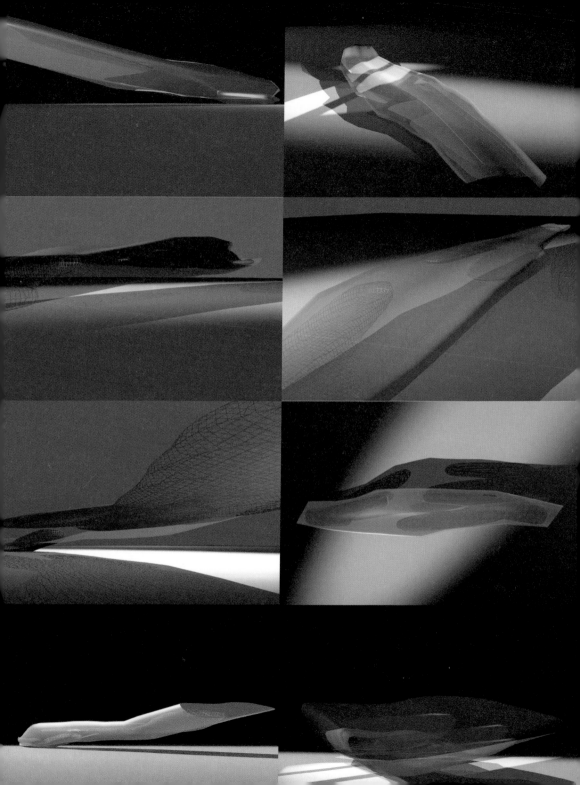

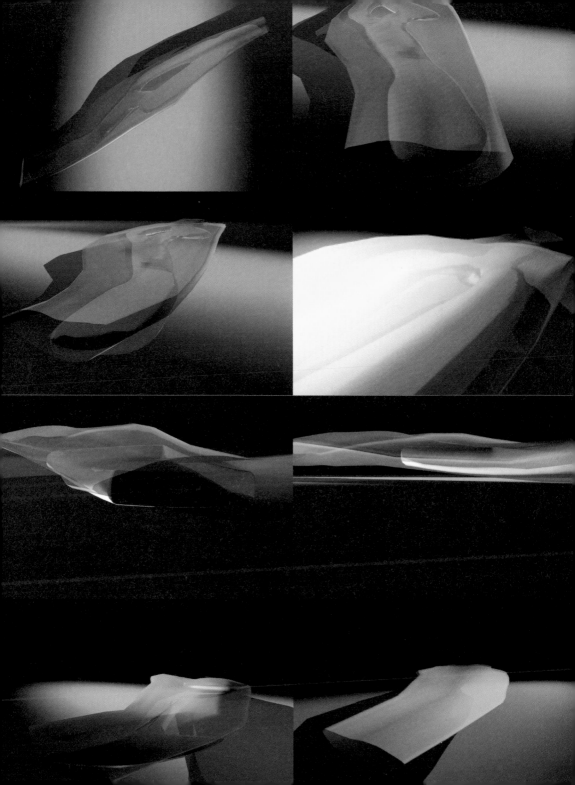

he project is based on the dynamic analysis of flux and
he study of its origins.
Europark II is divided into two parts: the expansion of the
existing shopping center and the landscape design of the area
surrounding the Europark.
The shopping center is divided into two storeys, two glazed
volumes that are penetrated by curved shapes and islands.
The car park at the roof level is covered by a variety of fluid
shapes recalling the islands below, which become the focal
points of the new complex.
The landscape design is organized according to the footpaths.
The leisure and child area consists of artificial hills,
pedestrian zones and raised areas built in timber, while the
bushes containing bamboo and other tall plants define a new
relationship between the buildings and the local geography.

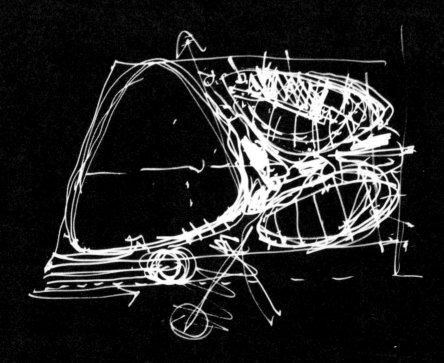

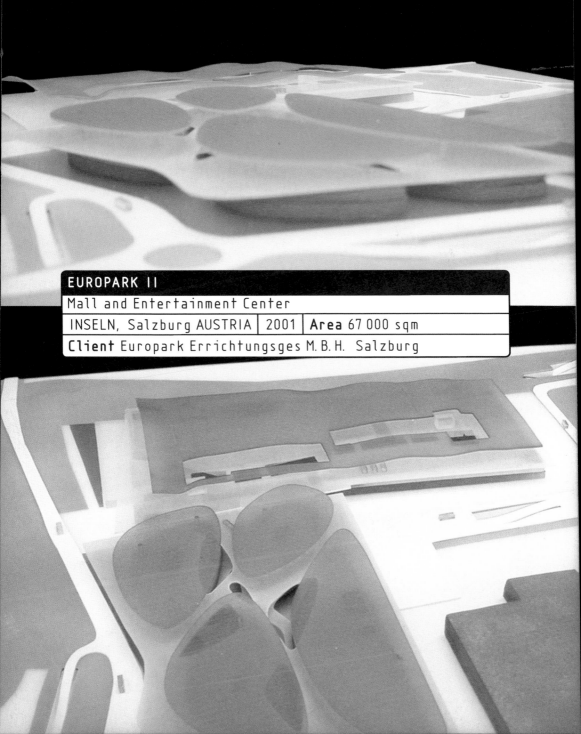

EUROPARK II

Mall and Entertainment Center

| INSELN, Salzburg AUSTRIA | 2001 | **Area** 67 000 sqm |

Client Europark Errichtungsges M. B. H. Salzburg

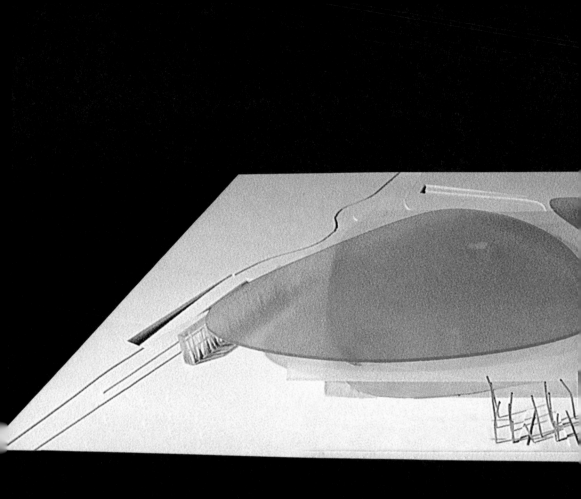

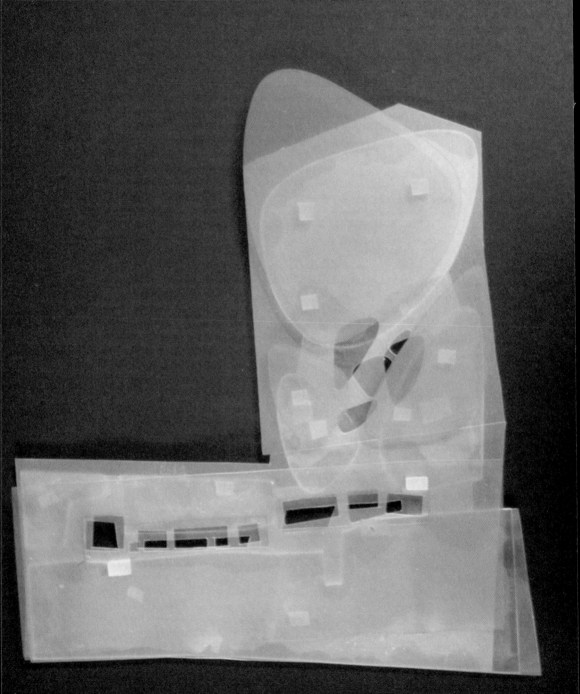

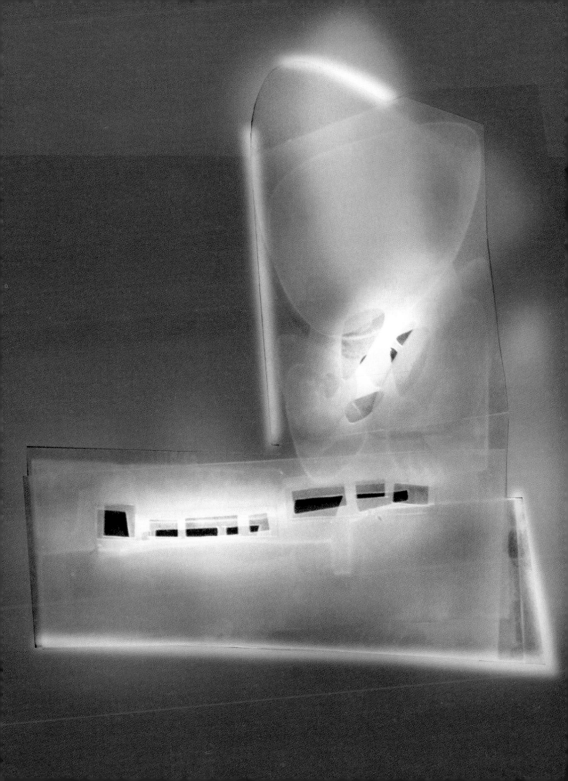

NEW CONCEPT FOR ARMANI

Armani shop, Café, Restaurant, Flower shop,		
cosmetics, bookshop	Hong Kong CHINA	2001
Area 2000 sqm	**Client** Giorgio Armani	

This project is a study in the concept of fluidity.
In fact it focuses on the routes taken by visitors
and their casual movements, and then builds a display
area around these invisible signs. According to a
traditional formalism of interior architecture,
the voids are more important than the fillings.
These flows are not decoration, they are the true
inspiration. Here the concept of a fashion display
area has been revolutionized and transformed into
a series of brightly lit lines that present clothes
and accessories from within two sheets of glass.
The intense luminosity of the lines varies, changing
the color of the surrounding area, as these are the
only form of illumination. We tried to create a space
in which everyone can feel like the only protagonist
inside a space designed only for him/herself.
The façade overlooking the street acts as a screen on
which fashion shows and collections can be projected
and interspersed with the myriad of city lights that
move and mutate endlessly.

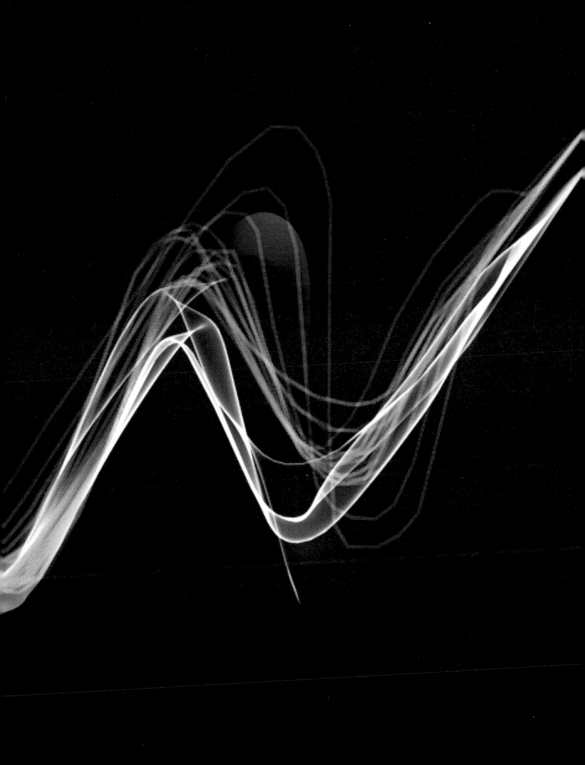

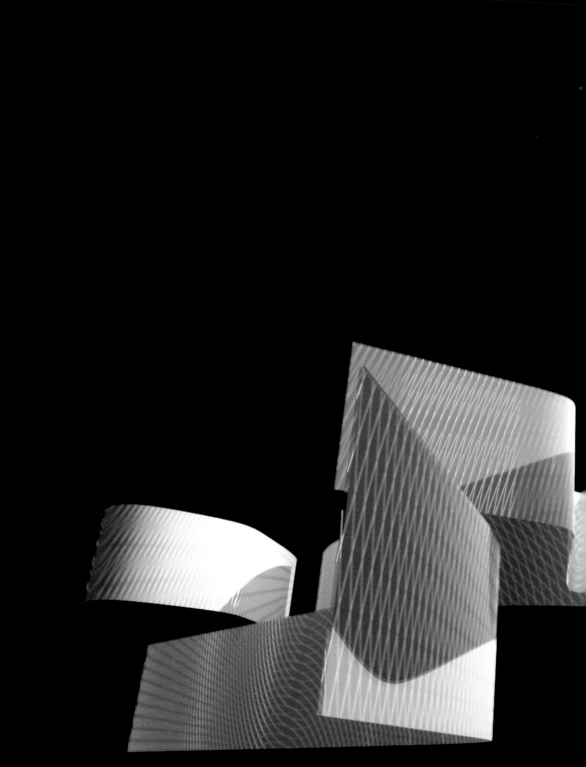

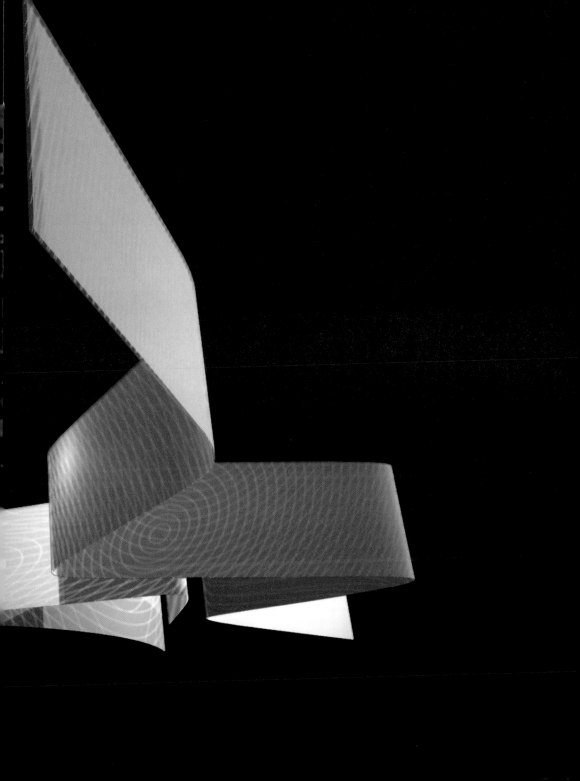

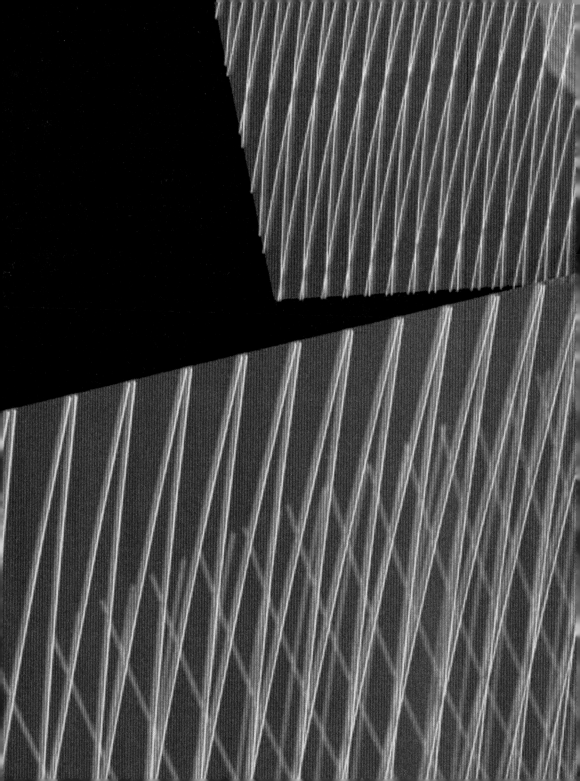

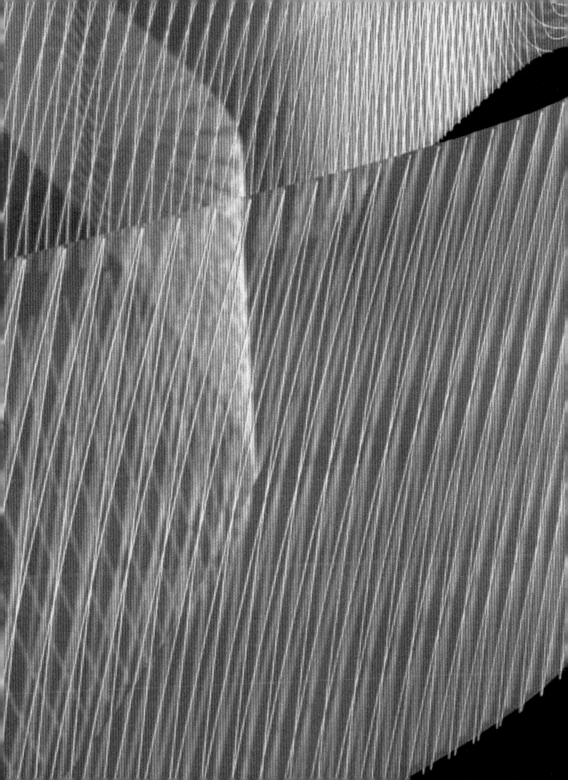

This experimental project, this reflection on the way in which our habits could be changed, was brought about by observing how technology has become part of our daily lives.
The idea is to apply the most refined and advanced technology in order to create a new concept of space, in this case a living area.
The new home, therefore, becomes a fluid and changeable membrane made of new materials. Thanks to the sensitivity of micro-sensors, it can change shape and adapt to the changing needs of its new resident, who is presumably immersed in the rapidity of Internet and hence, of communications and information.
It is an attempt to deform space and consider it truly dynamic and, therefore, functional in response to our new requirements, assuming that there is a real and direct interaction between people and their environment.

THIRD MILLENNIUM HOUSE

Bologna ITALY | 2000

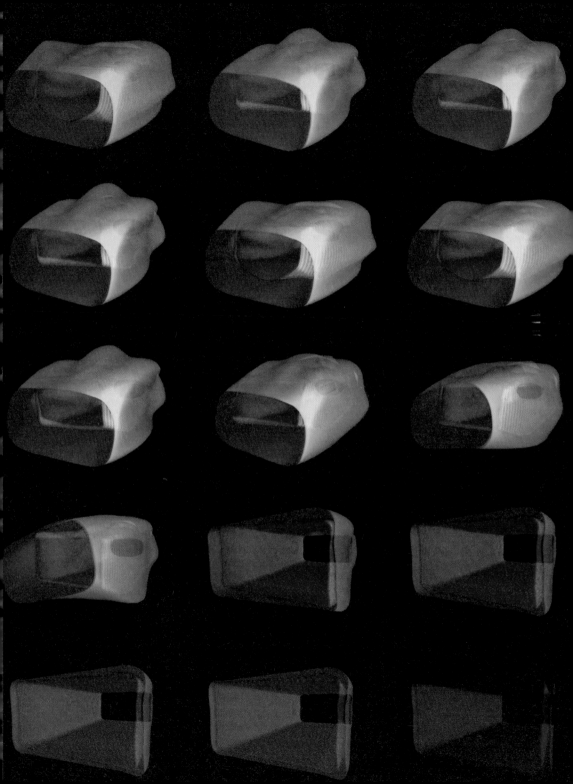

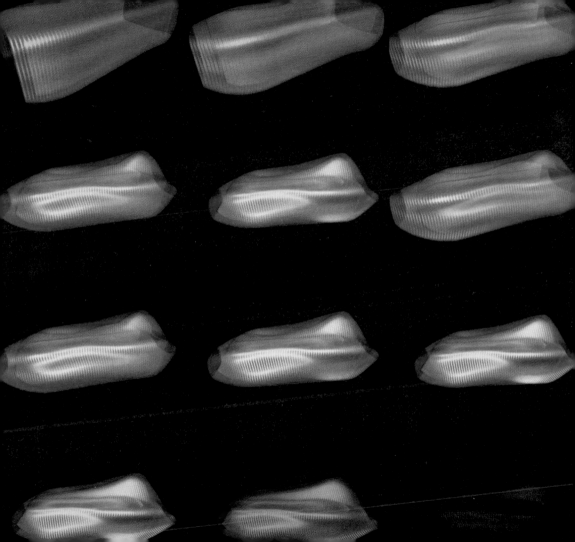

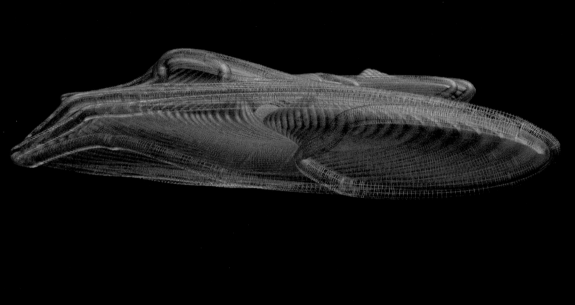

This is a study for a modern art gallery situated in a cultural zone that already exists. The new building must both integrate with and emerge from this pre-existing urban fabric.

The idea is to create a plaza which will connect, by means of a series of cultural walkways, the museum, the library and the new gallery that will become the real focus of interest.

From the bridge that joins this cultural complex to the city, visitors will be attracted by the outline of the building that changes continually as their viewpoint moves, creating powerful emotions already from a distance. When visitors reach the plaza they will feel so involved that they too will become part of the atmosphere created by the events going on around them.

The Gallery of Modern Art also creates a natural relationship between the cultural centre and the riverbank promenade.

The body of the building emerges almost violently from the riverbank giving visitors
the opportunity to enter caverns of light where the vitality of the piazza continues.

Natural light filters through the "pores" of the building giving the interior strength. Structural ribs wrap around the building in an east-west direction and sunlight enters through holes in the zenith to the north, making the display areas dynamic and flexible. The exhibition rooms areas and facilities are perceived as a single unit, even if the floor plans can be used in various different ways. The linearity of the interiors contrasts with the complexity of the shell creating a dissonance that plunges the spectator into the midst of the cultural activities.

Internal floors float at different heights underlining the free form of the external shell.

Ramps take visitors to the various levels creating the impression that they are floating in a void. On the lower floors the building seems almost to be trying to leave its mark by casting the shadow of its negative image on the ground.

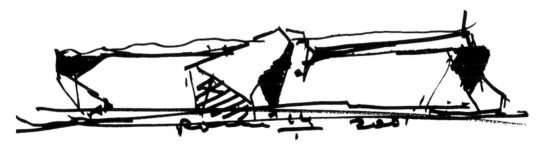

GALLERY OF MODERN ART
Study for a new concept of a modern art gallery | 2001

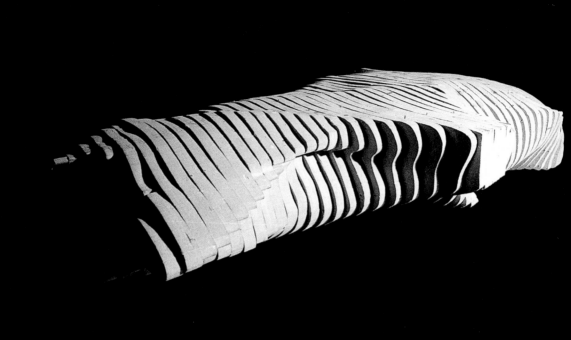

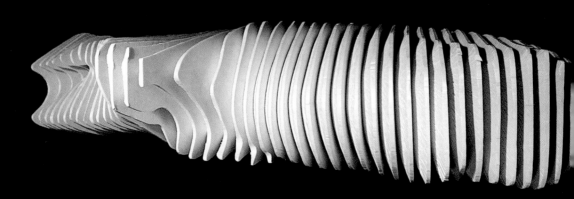

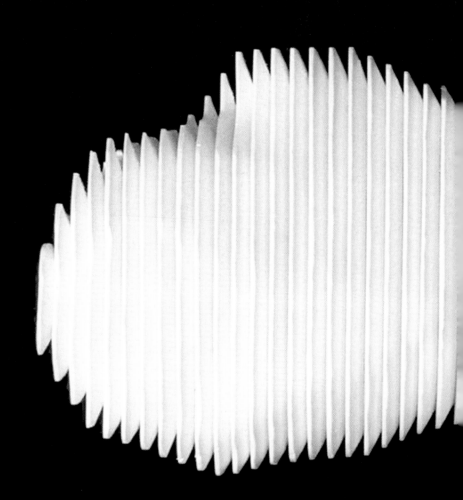

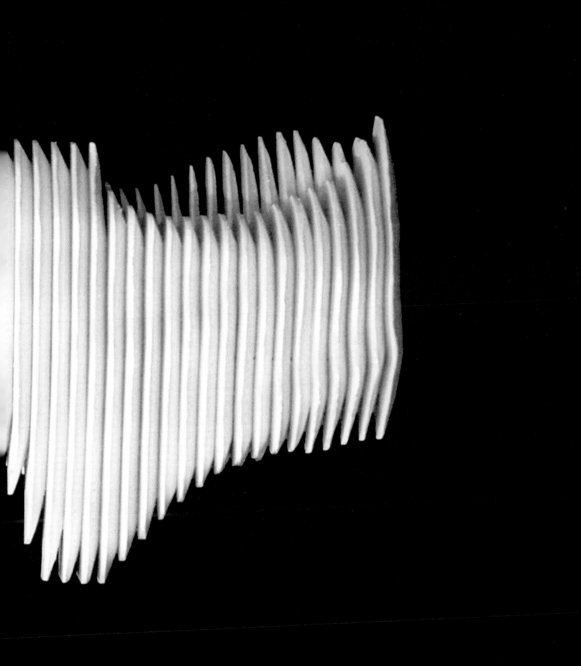

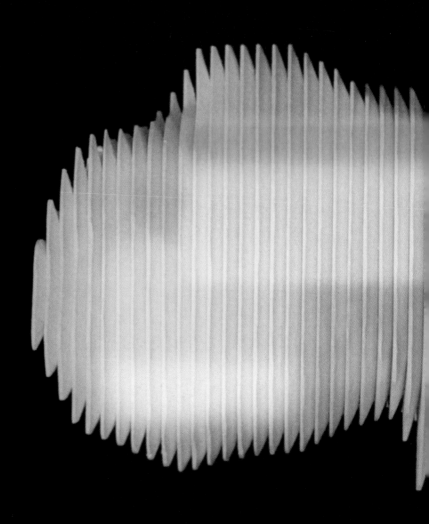

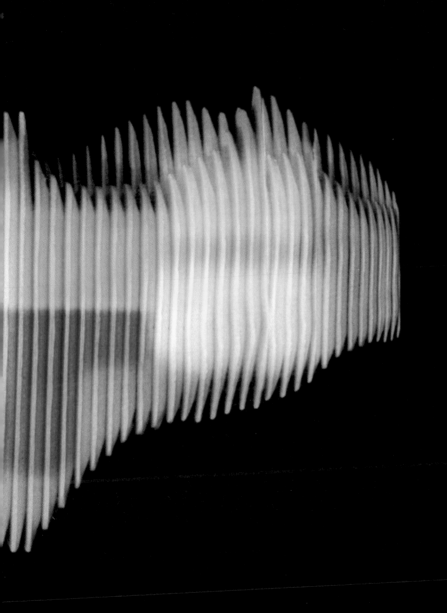

IT'S NOT ENOUGH / NON È ABBASTANZA

I have often asked myself what is the alchemy that makes all human beings so different. Some say psychoanalysis, others the enlightenment felt in front of an artwork or a famous building. Artists usually try to reconstruct their own history, but architects hardly ever do. I still do not understand what makes my profession of architect so unique. I only know that I didn't want to be one. I became an architect because my mother was afraid I would become an artist and, to her way of thinking, artists were people who never had any money. Anyway, I have never met God, or a psychoanalyst for that matter. I prefer other things. I can say that I decided to enter the architecture faculty in order to make my mother happy, but in fact it was a faculty that did not interest me in the least, it really did not excite me at all. My mother has always been very pragmatic, she was a philosophy teacher and always a communist. She was therefore convinced that her son must get a good degree. I did not really agree with her, I never have. I left home at the age of sixteen and went to school as usual, but painting was everything to me, it was the only thing that I really loved. So even it may seem paradoxical, I started university, without any desire whatsoever to become an architect. Only as time went by did I start to fall in love with this discipline. Anyway, when I started to study at the university, I did not know anything about architecture and that was terrible. In Italy an Architecture High School does not exist, there is only the University. A law dating back to the fascist period

established the creation of a faculty of architecture,
somewhere between Engineering and Fine Arts. The sum
of the two disciplines resulted in a course that was
ferociously difficult. There were 39 exams. 19 of these had
to be passed in the first two years, otherwise the student
was not admitted to the third year. Again, to keep my mother
happy, I took all the exams which was crazy. Despite all
this I knew nothing which shows that one can do anything
without knowing anything. There are hundreds of useless
exams. I finished them all, before the scheduled time too,
so I spent 6 months in Denmark. I visited Jorn Utzøn's
studio where I went back to work the following summer
and, at the same time, I began to look very carefully at
contemporary buildings. On the whole, I didn't think they
were that bad. When I came back, I wasn't so in love with
architecture anymore, but I began to do some work on the
subject. I read books, copied plans and cross sections.
I was simply trying to understand. The only subject I
was really interested in was the History of Architecture.
Contemporary art, on the other hand, was my life, my real
love. I have always refused to revere any master, but there
have been some people in my life that I am thankful to and
to whom I could dedicate many of my projects. The first is
Jurgis Baltrusaïtis, an art historian, known mainly for his
studies on anamorphosis and the fantasy world of the Middle
Ages. He was Lithuanian as well and, when I lived in Paris,
we used to meet frequently. I really liked seeing him as he
reminded me of my roots and I could speak to him using the
few words of Lithuanian that I still remember.

The other person I would like to remember is Giorgio
Caproni, one of the most important Italian contemporary
poets and one of the greatest translators of Céline.
His works have been translated all over the world.
He was my primary school teacher and I often used
to go to his house in the afternoon when school had
finished. We have always been very close. He played
the violin and adored electric trains that we often
assembled together. We built landscapes, while I read
him my poems, which were clearly those of a ten-year-old
child. I was mad about poetry and his world. Another
person I owe a lot to is Giorgio Castelfranco who I have
known since I was a child. I met many artists through
Castelfranco including Giorgio de Chirico who I worked
with for a while, in his studio in Piazza di Spagna.
At the time I did not feel alive if I didn't paint
every day. Anyway, I am sure that all my projects show
that my reference points certainly do not come from
architecture. My interests as well as my training have
always been closer to art. I love Burri, Fontana, Fluxus,
Gordon Matta Clark, Beuys, Arte Povera and Land Art,
the world of violence and poetry, the world of Krzysztof
Wodiczko and Pierpaolo Pasolini. In other words, I am
interested in becoming part of a process
that is different from the architecture in which we
live every day.
My real obsession is landscapes, like Ayers Rock, the red
mountain in Australia, the atolls in Polynesia, enormous
dunes that form and dissolve in the deserts, icebergs,

islands... I have always been fascinated by the beauty of
the absence of form, the imperfection of beauty. I have
always asked myself how it is possible to create a form
of architecture with no shape and with no geometrical
or complex dimensions.
This is why I believe that artists, even the worst ones,
are better than architects, because artists always start
from a vision, whereas architects never speak about it.
They always speak about a project.
My dream, on the other hand, is that everyone can have
ideas, passions and feelings. What is the point in
struggling to earn more and more, to gain more power?
In my opinion, capitalism and power are two concepts
that belong to the field of metaphysics. They are only
myths that exist to maintain their own myth. The human
situation is much less metaphysical. All of us try to
deal with it as best as possible. All of us try to find
solutions to the innumerable problems of everyday life.
We obviously can't dedicate all our daily energies to
politics or what is wrong with the system as we all have
difficult lives. We leave home in the morning and come
back at night. What can architecture do to help us live
better? It can say NO. This is obviously not particularly
revolutionary, but it does mean making certain choices
instead of others. Some time ago, a big investor asked
me to design a vast plan for 25 000 inhabitants next to
the Appia Antica, the great archaeological park.
I refused, but someone else who is said to be left wing,
accepted and the project was immediately approved.

TO REFUSE IS AT LEAST SOMETHING, AND EVERY TIME
WE SAY NO IS IMPORTANT.
We must always ask ourselves the same question: do we want
to give people what they ask for, that is to say, a world that
often has no taste or culture, or do we want to take the risk of
trying to create a better quality of life?
A man that I have always admired very much for the stands he
has taken and the courage of his choices, is Bruno Zevi, my
teacher at University. This is despite the fact that we have
always disagreed ever since I was a student. After years of
ups and downs, Zevi finally wrote an article where he admitted
that I at least had some merits. I called him up and, as usual,
he asked me to go to visit him, immediately! It was April 1995.
He was living in via Nomentana. I found him in good shape
in his dusty studio, surrounded as always by the most up to
date books. I tried embracing him even if he tried to stop
me with his usual, "I only hug women" (we embraced in any
case) and then he shot a question straight at me, point-blank.
"What are you going to do over the next ten years, apart from
architecture?" I have to say that it took me several weeks to
recover. The question asked in these terms doesn't have any
great answers, unless I start questioning much of what I have
done and thought over the years.
This attempt at savage psychoanalysis made me think a lot.
Perhaps it was this that influenced the choice of the theme
proposed for the 7th Venice Architecture Biennial Exhibition
2000: LESS AESTHETICS, MORE ETHICS.
Thinking about it again, I could also add,
"IT IS NOT ENOUGH, NON E' ABBASTANZA".

Major projects and realisations

1967 "Galdos" Cultural Center,
Las Palmas de Gran Canaria, Spain
1969 Flower Market, Pescia, Italy
1970 Rome Regional Council Pavilion, Rome
1970-1973 Sports Center, Sassocorvaro, Italy
1970-1971 Redeveloping and landscaping
an area previously used for dumping waste,
Tarquinia, Italy
1970 Exhibition design and layout for
the politico-satirical drawings with
Sebastian Matta, Tarquinia, Italy
1970-1971 Renovation of a private house, Rome
1970 Opera House, Belgrade, competition
1970 Georges Pompidou Center, Paris,
international competition
1970-1971 Private landscaping project, Rome
1972-1975 Residential complex,
Monte Livata, Italy
1972-1973 Office renovation, Rome
1972-1973 Private houses, Viterbo, Italy
1972-1974 Tourist center, Via Aurelia, Rome
1973-1983 Residential complex, Rome
1973 Artist's house and studio, Rome
1974 Skyscraper in the desert, Tunis,
international competition
1974-1975 Restoration and conversion of
"Monte Frumentario" into a cultural center,
Anagni, Italy
1974 Restoration of a private house,
Anagni, Italy
1974-1975 Restoration of Palazzo Moriconi,
Anagni, Italy
1974 School complex, Anagni, Italy
1975 Renovation of two medieval buildings,
Bolsena, Italy
1975 Private house, Rome
1975-77 Private house, Anagni, Italy
1976 Expansion of the cemetery, Paliano, Italy
1976 Head office complex, Florence, Italy,
international competition
1976-77 Private house, Acuto, Italy
1976-77 Restoration and expansion of
the old cemetery, Paliano, Italy
1977-78 "Fontana del Diavolo" park,
Paliano, Italy
1977-82 Nursery school and park,
Tarquinia, Italy,
with artistic intervention by Sebastian Matta
1977-79 New cemetery, Acuto, Italy
1977-81 New cemetery, Paliano, Italy

1977-80 Residential complex, Anagni, Italy
1979 Urban staircase, Paliano, Italy
1978-88 Secondary school complex, Anagni, Italy
1979-85 Gymnasium, Paliano, Italy
1979-86 Sports center, Anagni, Italy
1979-1982 Secondary school, Paliano, Italy
1979-1986 S. Giorgetto school complex,
Anagni, Italy
1980-83 "Ernica" residential complex,
Anagni, Italy
1980-90 New Town Hall complex, Cassino, Italy
1980-83 New Town Hall complex, Serrone, Italy
1980-82 Secondary school recreation area
(maze, theatre, observatory, and gardens)
Tarquinia, Italy
1982 Parc de la Villette, Paris,
international competition
1982-1984 Primary school,
Civita Castellana, Italy
1982-90 Private house, Civita Castellana, Italy
1982 Opéra Bastille, Paris,
international competition
1984-86 Cinema renovation and expansion,
Cotronei, Italy
1984-87 Residential complex, Paliano, Italy
1984-90 New cemetery, expansion, Paliano, Italy
1984-88 Cemetery expansion, Orvieto, Italy
1985-1989 New cemetery, Civita Castellana, Italy
1985-90 Renovation and extension of Piazza
Regina Margherita, Acquappesa, Italy
1985 Housing and artists' studios,
Seuilly, France
1985 La Promenade plantée, Bastille-Bois de
Vincennes, Paris, competition
1986 Five bus depots, Acotral, Rome, Viterbo,
Rieti, Frosinone, Latina, Italy
1986-89 Maison de la Confluence, Avoine, France,
competition, winning project
1986-91 Cultural and media center, Rezé, France
1986 European Tower: homes, offices, hotel,
Hérouville-Saint-Clair, France with
William Alsop, Jean Nouvel and Otto Steidle
1988-1991 Housing, sports center, gymnasium,
tennis courts, parking area, social and
commercial facilities and park,
Candie-Saint-Bernard, Paris, XI,
competition, winning project
1989 Renovation of the "Angélique-Trois Bornes"
residential complex, Saint-Ouen, France,
competition
1989 Town center renovation,
Cergy-Pontoise, France

1989 Processing plant for the conversion of
solid waste into methane gas, Nîmes, Francia,
competition, winning project
1989-93 Graffiti museum and grotto entrance,
Niaux, France, competition, winning project
1989 Renovation of the "Jardins de la Fontaine",
Nîmes, France, competition
1989 Urban plan for the station area of
Saint-Quentin-en-Yvelines, France,
competition, winning project
1989 Library, Alessandria, Eygpt,
international competition
1989 Arts, technology and media center,
Karlsruhe, Germany, international competition
1989-1991 Maison de la Communication et
du Câblage, Saint-Quentin-en-Yvelines, France,
competition, winning project
1990-95 University housing,
Herouville-Saint-Clair, France
1991 Conversion of the Casino and expansion of
the Grand Hôtel, Cabourg, France, competition
1991 Viaduct, town planning project,
Valmontone, Rome, competition, winning project
1991 Three office towers, houses and hotel,
La Part Dieu, Lyon, France
1991-92 Private house and studio, Cotronei, Italy
1991-93 Private house, Paris
1991 Castorama supermarket,
Hérouville-Saint-Clair, France
1991 Development plan for the Vauban Docks,
Le Havre, France
1991 Expansion of the ENITIAA, Nantes, France,
competition
1993 Renovation of the old harbour area,
Nagasaki, Japan, international consultancy
1991 International fashion center,
Tremblay-en-France, France
1991 Renovation of the banks of the Rhone river,
Valence, France, international consultancy
1991 Housing, shops and offices in the
old harbour area of Hamburg, Germany,
international competition, winning project
1991 Renovation of the "Les Minguettes" area,
Vénissieux, France, competition
1991 International Conference Center
"Quai Branly", Paris, France,
international competition
1991 National dance and musical conservatory,
Reims, France, competition
1991-99 Conversion of the former Aldobrandini
stables into the Tuscolo museum, cultural and
media center, Frascati, Italy

1991 Urban reclamation plan for of
the ex-Nalco area, Cisterna, Italy
1991 Renovation of the Bouilly-Pasteur sector of
the Cochin hospital, Paris, France, competition
1991 Offices and laboratories for
technical department facilities,
Valenton-Créteil, France, competition
1991 Renovation of the "Folies" quarter,
Saint-Germain-les-Arpajon, France, competition
1991 Renovation of the West entrance to the RN14,
France, consultancy, winning project
1991-93 Saint-Exupéry College, Noisy-le-Grand,
France, competition, winning project
1991 Renovation of two areas, 3/11
West India Dock road and 4-10 East Dock Road,
Docklands, London, international competition
1991-96 Restoration, expansion and
conversion of the Turgot Palace into the faculty
of Law and Economics, Limoges, France,
competition, winning project
1991 Redevelopment of the areas along the
bank of the river Seine, Clichy-la-Garenne,
France, competition, winning project
1991 Chamber of Commerce and Industry of
Nîmes-Uzès-Le Vigan, Nîmes, France,
competition, winning project
1991-93 Restoration , extension and conversion
of the "Couvent des Pénitents" into the European
Institute of Interior Design and Architecture,
students housing (INEAA), Rouen, France,
competition, winning project
1991 Renovation of the Luth area, Gennevilliers,
France, competition, winning project
1991-92 Ecole Nationale d'Ingénieurs et
Institut Scientifique (ENIB-ISAMOR), Technopole,
Brest, France, competition, winning project
1991 Expansion of the Law and Arts Research and
Education Department, Dijon, France, competition
1991 Town center renovation, Allonnes, France
1991 ENSMA (Ecole Nationale Supérieure de
Mécanique et Aéronautique, Futurscope,
Poitiers, France, competition
1991 Law, Economics and Science Research and
Education Department, Tours University,
France, competition
1991 Fuksas Associates Office,
Vicolo della Frusta, Rome
1991 Town center urban renovation,
Amiens, France, competition
1991-96 Restoration and extension of the "Hotel
Dieu" (Hospital for long term illness), Chartres,
France, competition, winning project

1991 A tower on 11 towers, "a collection along the river", Frankfurt, Germany, competition, winning project

1991 Offices, housing, shops in the old airport area, Munich, Germany, competition

1991 Urban renovation of the old station area, offices, housing, facilities, Frankfurt, Germany, competition

1991 Landscape plan for a 90 hectare area, Brétigny-sur-Orge, France, competition

1991 Urban renovation, Port-de-Bouc, Marseilles, France

1991-96 Sports complex, parking area, housing, shopping center and artists' studios for the R.I.V.P., Paris XI, competition, winning project

1991-96 Housing, offices and facilities along the Sprea, Berlin, Germany, competition

1991 Urban plan for the Lu Jiazui International Trade Center, Pudong, Shanghai, China, international consultancy

1992 Restoration and conversion of the "Gare du Prado" into an office, housing and shopping area, Marseilles, France, competition

1990-93 "Centre Ville" University documentation center, library and restaurant, Brest, France

1992-95 Redevelopment of the "Cité des Aigues Douces", Port-de-Bouc, France

1992 ZAC Berges-de-Seine, project for a new quarter, "Cables de Lyon", Clichy, France

1992 "Passerelle Solferino", a pedestrian bridge over the Seine, Paris, competition

1992 Congress center and extension of the Sheraton Hotel, Salzburg, Austria, competition

1992 Project for the renewal of the Castellazzo quarter. Restoration of the Villa Arconati Crivelli and surrounding areas. Forest and agriculture safeguarding project. Parking areas to aid the new road system. Bollate, Italy

1992 "Buero- und Gescaeftshaus Willhelmgalerie", Postdam, Germany, international competition

1992 Restoration and conversion of the old Zottmann Villa, into a museum for the Carnuntinum Museum Archaeological collections, Bad Deutsch-Altenburg, Austria, international competition

1992 Urban renovation of the railway station and surrounding area- Friedrichstrasse (housing, offices, facilities), Berlin, Germany, international competition

1992 Redevelopment of the "Domaine Bâti du Petit Arbois", in the Europole Méditerranéenne programme, Aix-Les-Milles, France, competition, winning project

1992 Urban and architectural renovation of the Town Hall area (Library and student's quarter), Limoges, France, competition, winning project

1992 Regional Center for Music and Voice, Argenteuil, France, competition

1992-95 Maison des Arts, exhibition center, multimedia center, ateliers, University of Bordeaux, France, competition

1992-96 Residential complex, Clichy-la-Garenne, France, competition

1992-97 Restoration of 4 towers built in the sixties, Montreuil, France

1993-02 Project for an international quarter in the Roissy airport, including TGV connections, RER Station (offices, shops, housing, university), Tremblay-en-France, France, competition, winning project

1993 Study for the reappraisal of the "Piazza dei Miracoli," Pisa, Italy, national competition

1993-95 Study for defining the urban layout of the old village center, Tremblay-en-France, France, competition

1994-1997 Europark Mall, entertainment center and parking area, Salzburg, Austria, international competition

1994 Covered Omnisports complex with open air sports facilities and underground carparks, Rueil – Malmaison, France, competition

1994 Reordering of the Alphonse Fiquet square. Renovation of the complex built by Auguste Perret, Amiens, France, international competition

1994 Master Plan for the areas south of the Agricultural and Food Center, Bologna, Italy, competition

1995 Urban redevelopment of the Neusser Strasse area, Monaco, Germany, international competition

1995 Proposals for the reutilization of the ex "Sudrum Leipzig" coal mines, Germany, international competition

1995 New "Caisse Française de Développement" headquarters, Paris, closed invitation competition, project mentioned

1995-98 "Maximilien Perret" College for the formation and research on construction, Alfortville, France, competition

1995 Feasibility study for the reordering of the Railway Station area, Padua, Italy

1995 Urban plan for the "Place des Nations", including design for the Maison Universelle, the new GATT headquarters, the central Library, two

Universities and research institutes, the "Maison des droits de l'homme et des droits humanitaires", and a center of worship for all religions, Geneva, Switzerland. Republic and Canton of Geneva, ONU, the Federal Government, international competition, winning project
1995 Feasibility study (offices) Wendenstrasse City-South, Hamburg, Germany, competition, winning project
1995 Urban and landscape study of the area surrounding the "Nordbahnhof", Berlin, Germany, closed invitation international competition
1995 Feasibility study for the planning of an administrative-residential area (housing, offices, school, nursery), Wienerbergstrasse/ Triesterstrasse, Vienna, Austria, international competition, winning project
1995-01 "Twin Tower", new Wienerberger headquarters including offices, multiplex, restaurants and underground carparks, Wienerbergstrasse, Vienna, Austria
1995 Offices, housing and a factory for the production and distribution of computers and software, Hamburg, Germany
1995 Fuksas Associates Office, Piazza del Monte di Pietà, Rome
1995 Urban and architectural plan for the Tiburtina and Tuscolana railway station areas and of the Tiburtina-Colombo connection highway, Rome, closed invitation international consultancy
1996 Football theme Park, Torvaianica, Italy
1996-99 Residential complex, Clichy, France
1997-98 Student housing and parking area, Alfortville, France
1997 Multimedia Center Rotherbaum, Hamburg, Germany, international competition
1997 12th Rome Quadrennial Exhibition of National Art layout design, Rome
1997 Central Library, Promenade des Arts, Nice, France, international competition
1997 Architectural redevelopment of the "Innsbruck Rathauspassage", Innsbruck, Austria, closed invitation international competition
1997 Charente Maritime "Hotel du Département", La Rochelle, France, closed invitation international competition
1997-00 Project for the restoration and functional redevelopment of the Termini Railway Station, Rome, Italy
1997 "Via Triumphalis" Urban plan for the Schloß- platz at the Karlsruhe Kongreszentrum, Germany, international competition

1997 Construction of a residential area in the old "Hindenburg-Kaserne" area at Münster, Germany, international competition
1997-01 Residential area and offices for the Hanseatica DWI, Hamburg, Germany
1997 Furniture for Saporiti Italia, Milan, with the collaboration of Doriana O. Mandrelli
1997-02 "Wohnen und Arbeiten am Alsterfleet" housing and offices, Hamburg, Germany
1997 New head management offices for the DEUTSCHE POST AG, Bonn, Germany, closed invitation international competition
1997 Synagogue, cultural center, offices, resden, Germany, international competition
1997 Functional renovation of the ex Aquarium and Theatre for Vittorio Gassman, Roma
1997 New "Caisse des Dépôts et Consignations" headquarters, Paris, France, closed invitation international competition
1998 Wohnungsbau Ost, Alte Messe Leipzig Town Urban redevelopment for converting part of the old fair in Lipsia into a residential complex, Lipsia, Germany, closed invitation international competition, winning project
1998-01 Renovation and expansion of housing and studios for artists, parking areas, for R. I. V. P, Paris, XIII, competition
1998-01 Peace Center, Jaffa, Israel, for Shimon Peres and Yasser Arafat
1998-02 New Fashion Pavilion at Porta Palazzo, Turin, Italy, closed invitation competition, winning project
1998 Brückenschlag und Reisegarten, Vlotho-Exter, Germany, international competition, winning project
1998 Neubau Büro Center am Axel-Springer-Platz, Hamburg, Germany
1998 "Staircase to the stars", Bethlehem, Palestine, for Yasser Arafat
1998 2 residential towers, Milan
1998 Water treatment plant, Caen, France, competition, winning project
1998 Marina di Stabia Tourist Port, Naples
1998 Urban redevelopment plan, Castellammare di Stabia, Naples
1999 Adidas "World of Sport", Hezogenaurach, Germany, international competition, project mentioned
1999-02 Redevelopment of "Piazza" Shopping Center and mall, Eindhoven, The Netherlands
1999 SWS Stadion, Salzburg Wals – Siezenheim, Salzburg, Austria, international competition, award winner

1999 Residential area, offices, shopping area, Pescara, Italy, international competition
1999 Residential complex, Brescia, Italy
1999 New Imperia railway station, Italy, closed invitation competition
1999 Sports center, Chalon sur Saone, France
1999-03 Hotel residential area and shopping center, Valenza Po, Italy
1999-03 Congress Center "ITALIA", EUR Rome, international competition, winning project
1999 New residential area containing public facilities and landscaped areas, Amiens, France, competition, winning project
1999 Residential area, offices and hotel, Schönbrunn , Vienna, international competition
1999 "Messe Zentrum" expansion, Salzburg, Austria, international competition
2000 TV-World, Hamburg, Germany, international competition, award winner
2000 Freizeit-und-Einkaufszentrum, Bern, Switzerland, international competition
2000-2002 Residential complex and shopping center, Rimini, Italy
2000 New Consiag headquarters, Prato, Italy, international competition, winning project
2000 Urban plan, Rogoredo, Italy
2000 Expansion of the WIPO World Intellectual Property Organization headquarters, Geneva, Switzerland, international competition, award winner
2000-2004 New Italian Space Agency headquarters, Rome, international competition, winning project
2000-2002 Mall and Entertainment Center, Belpasso, Catania, Italy
2000 Residential complex, offices, cinema and service sector, Brachmüle, Vienna, international competition, winning project
2000 Urban redevelopment of the "Source" quarter, Orléans, France, competition
2000 Gießereigelände workshop, Shopping Center, Conference Center, Hotel, Ingolstadt, Germany, international competition
2001 Queensland Gallery of Modern Art, Brisbane, Australia, international competition
2001 Justizzentrum, Aachen, Germany, international competition
2001 Center des Exposition et des Congres, Angouleme, France, international competition, winning project

2001-03 New Piedmont Region Council headquarters, Turin, Italy, international competition, winning project
2001 New Ferrari S. p. a. management offices and research platform, Maranello, Italy
2001-02 New concept for Armani with Doriana O. Mandrelli, Hong Kong, China
2001-03 San Giacomo parish complex, Foligno, Italy, international competition, winning project
2001 New headquarters for the publishing group Süddeutschen Verlages. Versand Auslbungstext, Munich, Germany, international competition
2001 Inner City development for Prague 2001 (Docks Prague 8) offices, mall, international competition
2001 Studienauftrag Theilerplat Landis and Gyr Areal und Sbb West, Zug, Switzerland, international competition, award winner
2001 Expansion of the mall and entertainment center, Europark II "Inseln" Salzburg, Austria
2001 Office building, Am Sandtorkai, Hamburg, Germany, international competition
2001 Study for a new concept of a Modern Art Gallery
2001 Waterfront reclamation and redevelopment, Hong Kong West, China, international competition
2002-04 Nuovo Polo Fiera di Milano, Padiglioni Espositivi, Centro Congressi, Uffici, Ristoranti, Parcheggi (per un'area di 700.000 mq), Milano, Italia.
2002-04 Konzept Freizeitbad Salzburg, Progettazione di un complesso di piscine, Salisburgo, Austria.

Monographies

LA SCUOLA MATERNA DI TARQUINIA
M. Fuksas, A.M. Sacconi, S. Matta
Carte Segrete Editions, Rome, January 1983

MASSIMILIANO FUKSAS, ANNA-MARIA SACCONI
Architetture 1971-1983,
Lille Architecture Faculty, 1983

SACCONI DA UNA CASA... A UN'ALTRA
Massimiliano Fuksas, Anna-Maria Sacconi
Carte Segrete Editions, Rome, June 1986

FUKSAS
Exhibition catalogue, Architecture Art Galerie
Geneva, April/May 1988
Drawings by Massimiliano Fuksas

FUKSAS, ARCHITETTO
Mario Pisani, Gangemi Editore, Rome, June 1988

HÉROUVILLE-SAINT-CLAIR, UNE TOUR EUROPÉENNE
Patrice Goulet, Carte Segrete Editions, Rome 1988

MASSIMILIANO FUKSAS, BLUE LAGOON N°6
Achille Bonito Oliva
Carte Segrete Editions, Rome 1990

MASSIMILIANO FUKSAS
Hambourg, Patrice Goulet
Carte Segrete Editions, Paris 1990

FUKSAS, BLUE TOWN
Antonella Greco
Carte Segrete Editions, Rome 1990

LA & AILLEURS, VINGT-CINQ ANNEES D'ARCHITECTURE
Massimiliano Fuksas
by Jeanne-Marie Sens & Hubert Tonka
Photographs by Doriana O. Mandrelli, Ombre Vive
Pandora Editions, Paris 1991

LA MAISON DE LA COMMUNICATION
by Massimiliano Fuksas
at Saint-Quentin-en-Yvelines
Jeanne-Marie Sens & Hubert Tonka
Photographs by Georges Fessy
Pandora Editions, Paris 1991

MASSIMILIANO FUKSAS 60 PROJETS
Patrice Goulet, Institut Français d'Architecture
Carte Segrete Editions, Rome 1992

FUKSAS DOWNTOWN 1992-94
Conception et réalisation: Giovanna Bellant
Carte Segrete Editions, Rome 1994

MASSIMILIANO FUKSAS
Neue Bauten und Projekte / Recent Buildings and
Projects, preface by John Welsh
Artemis Verlag AG Editions, Zurich 1994

MASSIMILIANO FUKSAS, UN JOUR...UNE VILLE !
Conférences d'Architectes
Pavillon de l'Arsenal 1994/1995
Pavillon de l'Arsenal Editions

MASSIMILIANO FUKSAS, OSCILLAZIONI E SCONFINAMENTI
Ruggero Lenci for the Universale di Architettura
(Series supervised by Bruno Zevi)
Graf Art - Officine Grafiche Artistiche
Venaria (Turin), July 1996

MASSIMILIANO FUKSAS, ONE. ZERO ARCHITECTURES
by Doriana O. Mandrelli and Massimo Riposati
Editoriale Giorgio Mondadori, Rome, June 1997

MIDDLE AGE
Progetti e architetture di Massimiliano Fuksas
DADART Virtual Gallery
by Pino Brugellis and Doriana O. Mandrelli
Florence, February 1997
www.fuksas.it

MASSIMILIANO FUKSAS
by Francis Rambert
Editions du Regard, Paris, November 1997

MASSIMILIANO FUKSAS
for CAW Contemporary World Architects
introduction by James Wines
Rockport Publishers
Gloucester, Massachusetts in two versions:
English and Japanese, January 1998

MASSIMILIANO FUKSAS. OCCHI CHIUSI, OCCHI APERTI,
Alinea Editrice srl, Florence, March 2001

MASSIMILIANO FUKSAS
with Paolo Conti, CAOS SUBLIME
Rizzoli, Milan, May 2001

TWIN TOWER
Wienerbergstraße 11, VIENNA, AUSTRIA
Architect Massimiliano Fuksas
Studio Fuksas Roma
Project Supervisors Alessandro Casadei,
Antoine Hahne
Project Team Carmelo Baglivo,
Frederica Caccavale, Riccardo Crespi, Filippe
Lozano, Lalinde, Till Noske, Katja Onori,
Christine Schenck, Matthias Schmidt-Rabenau
Studio Fuksas Vienna
Project Supervisor Ralf Bock
Project team Johannes Behrens, Stefano Bruno,
Eva-Ursula Faix, Marina Kavalirek, Zoltan Kiss,
Jaqueline Mandl, Benedikt Schwering
Client Immofinanz Immobilien Anlagen AG, Vienna
(A), Wienerberger Baustoffindustrie AG, Vienna (A)
Structural Consultants BŸro Thumberger +
Kressmeier, Vienna, (A)

URBAN DEVELOPMENT OF THE LU JIAZUI TRADE CENTER,
PUDONG, SHANGHAI, CHINA
Architect Massimiliano Fuksas
Project Supervisors Rikuo Nishimori,
Goedele Desmet
Project team P. Anania, G. Bellaviti,
B. Tulkens, M. Viederman, S. Agostino
Consultants Doriana O. Mandrelli,
Jean Michel Roux
Model Makers J. Kirimoto, C. Dattilo

WATER FRONT RECLAMATION AND REDEVELOPMENT,
HONG KONG WEST, CHINA
Architect Massimiliano Fuksas
Project Team Fabio Cibinel, Giorgio Martocchia,
Tiago Mota Saraiva
Model Makers Gianluca Brancaleone, Andrea
Marazzi, Angel Gaspar Casado, Nicola Cabiati
Client Government Hong Kong

MAXIMILIEN PERRET DE VINCENNES,
COLLEGE FOR THE FORMATION AND
RESEARCH ON CONSTRUCTION,
Rue des Goujons, ALFORTVILLE, FRANCE
Architect Massimiliano Fuksas
Project Supervisors Patrizia Anania, Ani Armagan
Project Team Juan Machado, Assunta Viola
Site Supervisors Romain Reuther, Eric Villenave
Client Ile de France Regional Council
Model Makers Claudia Dattilo

EUROPARK MALL, ENTERTAINMENT CENTER,
Europastraße 1, SALZBURG, AUSTRIA
Architect Massimiliano Fuksas
Project Supervisors Ralph Bock, Suzanne GrŸner
Project team Concetta Schepis, Dietmar Haupt,
Juan Machado, Junia Sato, Stefano Delisi,
Assunta Viola, Richard Lanning, Patrizia Anania,
Federico Tranfa, Gianfranco Di Gregorio
Client SPAR Warenhandels AG,
Salzburg Consultants
Engineering Vasko & Partners

REDEVELOPMENT OF "PIAZZA SHOPPING CENTER AND MALL"
18, Septemberplein 5, EINDHOVEN, THE NETHERLANDS
Project Supervisors Gijs Pyckevet. Tom Broekaert
Design Team Kristian Sullivan, Michele Crò,
Fiorenza Polacchi, Taymoore Balbaa,
Carmen Peña, Julia Lindenthal, Michael Stahlmann,
Tiago Mota Saraiva
Client William Properties BV., Rodamco,
Nederland, NV
Model Makers Marco Frugoni, Adriano De Gioannis
Consultants Van Moort en Partners
Architecten BV., Advies bureau Tielemans
Adviesbureau H. O. R. I.

NEW FERRARI MANAGEMENT OFFICES AND
RESEARCH PLATFORM MARANELLO, ITALY
Project Massimiliano Fuksas
Project Supervisor Giorgio Martocchia
Design Team Adele Savino, Fabio Cibinel,
Dario Binarelli, Laura Pistoia, Motohiro Takada,
Agostino Ghirardelli, Alessandro Mascia,
Tiago Mota Saraiva, Alessandra D'amico,
Francesco Anzolin
Model Makers Marco Galofaro, Nicola Cabiati
Gianluca Brancaleone
Client FERRARI S. p. a
System Installation Consultants
AI Engineering, Turin
Structure Studio Sarti, Rimini

"SAN GIACOMO" PARISH COMPLEX, FOLIGNO, ITALY
Project Massimiliano Fuksas
Project Team Fabio Cibinel, Giorgio Martocchia
Taymoore Balbaa, Tiago Mota Saraiva
Model Makers Marco Galofaro, Gianluca Brancaleone
Client Diocesi di Foligno,
Conferenza Episcopale Italiana

PEACE CENTER. JAFFA, ISRAEL
Project Massimiliano Fuksas
Design Team Alessandro Casadei,
Fabrizio Bastoni, Kristian Sullivan,
Taymoore Balbaa, Tiago Mota Saraiva
Model Makers Marco Galofaro,
Angel Gaspar Casado, Andrea Marazzi,
Takumi Saikawa, Giancarlo Poli, Miguel Mesa
Client Shimon Peres

7th INTERNATIONAL ARCHITECTURE EXHIBITION
"LESS AESTHETICS MORE ETHICS"
VENICE BIENNIAL EXHIBITION 2000
Director Massimiliano Fuksas
Videoinstallation 284m x 5m
Screenplay and direction Massimiliano Fuksas,
Doriana O. Mandrelli

MALL & ENTERTAINMENT CENTER. BERN, SWITZERLAND
Project Massimiliano Fuksas
Project Team Fabio Cibinel, Chiara Baccarini,
Hector Mendoza, Francesco Sacconi,
Taymoore Balbaa
Model Makers Marco Galofaro, Michael Shevel,
Gianluca Brancaleone, Yumiko Kimura
Client Genossenshaft Mingros Aare

CONGRESS CENTER "ITALIA" EUR. ROME, ITALY
Project Massimiliano Fuksas
Project Supervisor Lorenzo Accapezzato
Project Team Alessandro Casadei, Fabio Cibinel,
Fabio Barillari, Riccardo Gaggi, Luca La Torre,
Kristian Sullivan, Chiara Baccarini,
Dario Binarelli, Filipe Boin, Alessandra D'amico,
M. Teresa Facchinetti, Tobias Hegermann,
Keiko Nogami, Adele Savino, Fabio Semprini,
Motohiro Takada
Client EUR S. p. a.
Model Makers Gianluca Brancaleone,
Nicola Cabiati, Marco Frugoni, Marco Galofaro,
Takumi Saikawa, Angel Luis Gaspar Casado,
Andrea Marazzi
System Installation Consultants
AI ENGINEERING, Turin
Halcrow group Leeds, UK
Structure STUDIO MAJOVIECKI, Bologna, Italy
PROGES ENGINEERING, Rome
Acoustics XU- Acoustique, Paris, France

NEW ITALIAN SPACE AGENCY HEADQUARTERS
Project Massimiliano Fuksas
Project Supervisor Lorenzo Accapezzato
Project Team Fabio Cibinel, Simona Martino,
Riccardo Gaggi, Chiara Baccarini
Dario Binarelli, Alessandra D'amico,
M. Teresa Facchinetti, Cristina Gagliardi,
Keiko Nogami, Motohiro Takada
Client Agenzia Spaziale Italiana
Model Makers Marco Galofaro, Takumi Saikawa,
Alessandra D'amico, Keiko Nogami
System Installation Consultants
AI Engineering, Turin, Italy
Structure Progres Engineering, Rome

NEW PIEDMONT REGIONAL COUNCIL HEADQUARTERS.
TURIN ITALY
Project Massimiliano Fuksas
Project Team Fabio Cibinel, Federica Caccavale,
Giorgio Martocchia, Dario Binarelli,
Laura Pistoia, Simona Martino
Client Piedmont Regional Council
Model Makers Marco Galofaro, Nicola Cabiati,
Andrea Marazzi, Tiago Mota Saraiva,
Gianluca Brancaleone
System Installation and Structural Consultants
AI Engineering, Turin, Italy

SWS STADIUM SALZBURG WALS-SIEZENHEIM,
SALZBURG, AUSTRIA
Project Massimiliano Fuksas
Project Team Fabio Cibinel, Fabio Barillari,
Fabio D'Agnano
Model Makers Takumi Saikawa
Client SWS Wals-Siezenheim

ADIDAS "WORLD OF SPORTS",
HERZOGENAURACH, GERMANY
Architect Massimiliano Fuksas
Project Team Fabio Cibinel, Eva Schenk,
Alessandro Casadei, Takumi Saikawa
Model Makers Alberto Francini,
Lorenzo Accapezzato
Client Adidas

EXPANSION OF THE MALL AND ENTERTAINMENT CENTRE, EUROPARK INSELN, SALZBURG, AUSTRIA

Project   Massimiliano Fuksas
Project Supervisor   Tobias Hegemann
Project Team   Chiara Baccarini,
Agostino Ghirardelli, Michael Iovanel,
Michael Stahlmann
Model Makers   Angel Gaspar-Casado, Nicola Cabiati
Client   Europark Errichtungsges M. B. H.   Salzburg

NEW CONCEPT FOR ARMANI, HONG KONG, CHINA

Project   Massimiliano Fuksas and
Doriana O. Mandrelli
Project Team   Davide Stolfi, Motohiro Takada,
Defne Dilber, Iain Wadham
Client   Giorgio Armani
Model Makers   Angel Gaspar-Casado, Gianluca
Brancaleone, Nicola Cabiati, Andrea Marazzi

STUDY FOR THE THIRD MILLENNIUM HOUSE

Bologna 2000
Project   Massimiliano Fuksas
Project Team   Fabio Cibinel
Consultants   Doriana O. Mandrelli,
Giuseppe Brugellis

NEW CONCEPT FOR A CONTEMPORARY ART GALLERY

Project   Massimiliano Fuksas
Project Team   Fabio Cibinel, Chiara Baccarini,
Giorgio Martocchia, Michael Stahlmann
Model Makers   Andra Marazzi

TV COMMERCIAL

Agency   Publicis
Client Service Director   Jean Lamberti
Account Executive   Gabriele Moratti
Client   Renault Italia
Product   Scénic
Formats   45", 30", 150"
Subject   FUKSAS
Payoff   Non c'è mai una sola strada.
Art Director   Elena Carrozza
Copywriter   Domenico Di Lorenzo
For the Client Lapo Brogi
Advertising Service Chief
Media Specialist   Angelo Bencivenga
Advertising Executive   Francesco Zampagliene
Production House   BRW
Director   Thed Lenssen
For the Fuksas Studio   Giuseppe Brugellis
The pictures of Massimiliano Fuksas' projects are
taken from the FILMAC videos, (Filippo Macelloni)
The images taken from the Magma City video were
produced by RAI SAT ART.